Life Is BeauTEALful

Lessons from an Ovarian Cancer Survivor

> I can shake off everything as I write.
> My sorrows disappear, my courage is reborn.
> —Anne Frank

Copyright ©2022 Paula W. Millet

All rights reserved

No part of this book may be reproduced in any form, including electronic or mechanical means, without written consent of the publisher
ISBN: 978-0-9976677-7-6
Cover photo – Getty Images
Second Chapter Publishing
White, Georgia 30184
Your questions or comments are welcomed:
paulawmillet@gmail.com
For information on other books by the author or to follow the blog visit her website:
Paulamillet.com

Table of Contents

The Nomads --- *1*
Cover Story --- *3*
Celebrating Small Victories -- *8*
My Magical Month --- *11*
Excuse my Absence -- *15*
The Prescription --- *18*
The Language Lesson -- *22*
Saying Goodbye to Boudreaux -- *25*
The Mystery Cat -- *28*
The Cat, Part II --- *32*
Saving Things for Good --- *34*
Would you Like Some Cheese with that Whine? -------------------- *37*
Kindness Matters --- *41*
The Party -- *44*
To Rest -- *47*
The Thankful Book -- *50*
The Perfectly Imperfect Holiday -------------------------------------- *56*
Twelve Months of Good Intentions ------------------------------------- *59*
The Twelfth Night -- *65*
Words that Start with a C, Part I ------------------------------------ *68*
Part II -- *70*
Yet Another Cat Story -- *72*
Let's Agree to Disagree -- *76*
It's Carnival Time --- *79*
V is for Virus --- *81*
I is for Inspiration --- *85*
Angelique's World -- *89*
Developing Immunity -- *101*
The Peonies -- *105*
Can We Talk? --- *108*

Readers, Reviews, and Rock 'n Roll	112
2020 Vision	115
Happy Father's Day	118
Cancerversary Number Three	121
Unplugged	124
Deadly Disasters	127
Scan Day	129
Third Time's the Charm	133
Let There Be Light	135
I'm Not Old: I'm an Antique Little Girl	138
Take My Hand	146
The Good Patient	149
Begin with the End in Mind	152
The Update: I Wasn't Prepared	156
The Reprieve	161
Let There Be Paint	164
What I Learned as I Recovered from Surgery	166
The Last Jar of Jelly	171
The Gift of Life	174
Thanksgiving Traditions	178
This Christmas is Different	181
The Resolution Ritual	184
What's Behind Us and Before Us	188
The Law of Scarcity	192
Groundhog's Day	196
I Can See	200
Back in the Saddle Again	204
My Trip to Paris	208
We Wear the Mask	212
My Brave Face	215
And So We Meet	220
My 4th Cancerversary	224
Planting Hope	231

- The Notebooks (with my apologies to Nicholas Sparks) --------- 235
- Stuck in Second Gear --------- 239
- It's Been Cancelled --------- 243
- The Fear Factor --------- 248
- Lessons from a Hummingbird --------- 251
- Lost in a Forest --------- 253
- Decisions, Decisions --------- 257
- The Tears --------- 260
- Let's Have a Margarita --------- 264
- Lighten the Load --------- 269
- Don't Leave me Behind --------- 272
- In the Hospital --------- 274
- The Science of Writing --------- 277
- Embracing the New Year --------- 280
- It's a Snow Day --------- 282
- Remembering Lola --------- 285
- The Five Stages of Cancer --------- 290
- Chasing Waterfalls --------- 294
- Love Thyself --------- 297
- The Foundation --------- 301
- The Gratitude Lesson --------- 304
- Perception --------- 307
- The Peak End Rule --------- 310
- What I Learned from a Puritan Poet --------- 312
- Something to Leave Behind --------- 314
- The Miracle --------- 317
- God, The Father --------- 321
- My Momma Could Fold a Fitted Sheet --------- 325
- The Broken Vase --------- 327
- The Road Traveled --------- 330
- The Power of the Moment --------- 332
- Author's Notes: --------- 335

The Nomads

One night a group of nomads were preparing to unroll their sleeping mats when suddenly they were surrounded by a great light. As they stood transfixed, they knew that they were in the presence of a celestial being. With great anticipation, they awaited a heavenly message of great importance that they knew must be especially for them.

Finally, a voice spoke. "Gather as many pebbles as you can. Put them in your saddle bags. Tomorrow will find you glad, but it will also find you sad."

After having departed, the nomads shared their disappointment with each other. They had expected the revelation of a significant universal truth that would enable them to create wealth, health and purpose for the world. But instead they were given the menial task that made no sense to them at all. However, the memory of the brilliance of their visitor caused each one to pick up a few pebbles and deposit them in their saddlebags before retiring for the night.

They woke the next morning and while breaking up their camp to continue on their journey, they reached into their saddlebags and discovered that every pebble they had gathered had become a diamond. They were glad they had diamonds; they were sad that they had not gathered more pebbles.

I love this legend. I'm not quite sure where I first heard it, perhaps long ago in one of those illustrated fairy tale books, but it has been my go-to, first day of school opening for every class I have ever taught. I used to link it to learning with the pebbles being nuggets of knowledge that I hoped each student would gather during our time together. But today, I share it with you because it's a fine philosophical view of life. Experience all that you can while you are here on God's green earth. Moments, even the challenging or ordinary ones, may seem like pebbles, but someday you will see their value. Embrace every opportunity that comes to you. Like those sparkling gems, this life is precious. So precious.

And as you read through this book, I hope that like the nomads, you will see the value in each story, which spans year three, four, and five of my cancer fight. When I released *Ovacoming* and *Still Ovacoming*, I considered my writing mission complete. Quite frankly, I didn't think there was much more to learn along the way. I was wrong. And I am pleased to share those lessons with you here.

Cover Story

An Excerpt From *Ovacoming*: The Blue Butterflies

I particularly like butterflies. Several blue ones visit me daily, and on most summer mornings, they land outside the bedroom door, slowly flapping their wings in recognition. I find their presence comforting. I would even go so far as to say that I have come to view them as heavenly messengers since their first appearance here coincided with a visit from my sister-in-law, who at the time was battling late stage ovarian cancer. And no, the irony is not lost on me.

When I penned *Angelique's War*, I wanted an angelic symbol that I could carry throughout the novel. And the blue butterfly was perfect, of special significance to me, and hopefully, to my readers as well. It is hard to forget the haunting image of a beautiful creature gracefully landing on the outstretched finger of an innocent five-year-old girl, desperate to find her way back home.

I even planted a special bush in my yard, one that is known to attract them. I wanted to create a happy environment, although I have no idea if butterflies experience such emotions. It simply seemed like a nice reciprocal gesture in appreciation for the many hours of joy that they had brought me. And yes, I guess I am getting a little carried away with the personification here. Forgive me as I over-explain why they are special to me. I feel that it is important to do so before I write this next part.

You know, most kindergarteners can relate the basic story of how a caterpillar becomes a colorful butterfly. And we have often used the term metamorphosis to describe any kind of major transformation. But few people know what really happens during this process. I recently learned of it myself and found their evolution absolutely fascinating.

If you have ever had a garden, you have probably battled the lowly caterpillar as it chomps its way through your prized foliage. It eats hundreds of times its weight in a day until stuffed and bloated, it hangs itself up to recover. Its skin begins to harden, forming a chrysalis, a temporary house of sorts for the creature. But there, deep inside the caterpillar's body, things are changing as it begins to produce what entomologists call imaginal discs. Now, the poor insect's immune system doesn't recognize these invaders and tries to attack them. But they continue to produce at an alarming rate, eventually linking together. The caterpillar's resistance is compromised, making it unable to fight the stress, and its protection fails, while the stronger imaginal discs convert into imaginal cells that build the butterfly. As the caterpillar dies and decomposes, the butterfly feeds on that which remains until it is strong enough to emerge in its new form.

Admittedly, it is a bit gruesome, but also amazing, a biological marvel. And yes, the caterpillar must die in order to give the butterfly life. Gee, that makes for a great metaphor.

Cancer is also an attack on the immune system. There is a similar internal battle being fought as the good and bad cells arm wrestle for power, with life or death hanging in the balance. We are given chemo therapy, which destroys both the healthy and malignant tissue, anticipating that the body will eventually recover enough to keep the evil interlopers at bay. Ok, that's a bit simplistic, but close enough to prove the point.

What most folks, including the medical community, fail to fully realize is that the siege is not just physical. Cancer packs an emotional and psychological wallop as well. With the diagnosis comes a signed certificate of uncertainty, delivered by the Grim Reaper himself. You slap a smile on your face and claim to be doing well, while the scared child inside is screaming. You focus on trying not to fall apart in public places. You hide a lot of the anxiety, shielding others from your reality. That's the truth. And only part of the story.

But if you are able to make it past those first months of shock and despair, if you are able to survive the consequences of treatment, you begin to discover unexpected rewards, the emotional pot of gold. Most of these come in the form of spiritual growth. Let's face it: even the most avowed atheist sometimes calls out to God when faced with his own mortality. For the believer, there is the healing and comfort that accompanies faith. The resulting peace of acceptance is empowering. But more importantly, you come to understand that sometimes we have to release the old to embrace the new. You see, a diagnosis like cancer changes you forever. But once you gain the necessary clarity to understand what that change truly means in your life, you can see that there is a fullness of heart, a sense of pure joy. The scenery is quite lovely on the other side of the mountain. And so, what starts out as an end can actually be a beginning. I know this much is true.

When we believe we have all the time in the world, when life seems limitless, we hold ourselves back, whispering "not now, not yet" in the inner dialogue that examines our dreams. We are held tightly in place by that which is safe and familiar. We censor our thoughts and emotions, careful about what we reveal of ourselves to others, fearful that we won't be understood or accepted. But when the days are possibly numbered, we somehow give ourselves permission to take risks, to authentically stand in our own truth. Fueled by a sense of urgency, the confines fall away. And in the process, we learn how to live. Like the caterpillar, we become transformed through the pain and suffering. We struggle to emerge, clothed in a new garment that somehow fits us better. And then, in the blink of an eye, we spread our wings and fly.

Celebrating Small Victories

Slot machines are calibrated to celebrate small wins, while glossing over the small loses. If you have ever spent any time in a casino, you'll understand what I mean. A buck or two added to the "credit pot" will unleash a whole series of music and bells, while a forfeiture of that same amount results in silence. Of course, there is a psychology to this, based on research into how the human mind reacts to taking chances.

And while I don't gamble (I shop: it's a sure thing), there is something to be learned here. Our human brain seems to be programmed to think in an opposite way.

We often tend to focus on our missteps and stumbles as we make our way down the road of life, seeing them as major events, while failing to celebrate the small triumphs, the tiny moments of joy that we often overlook. Most people can recall, in vivid detail, an embarrassing scenario from the seventh grade, while dismissing the simple words of affirmation offered by a boss in passing. We focus on the annoying little family spats without looking for the days of positive interaction and shared laughter.

Is that human nature at work or cultural conditioning? We are admonished at every turn to "go big or go home." And so we hang our heads when we fall short of the big goal, the major prize. Is walking that first mile after years of being sedentary less spectacular than running a marathon? Is planting one tomato less rewarding than cultivating a big garden? Maybe. But if all we are able to focus on is the big prize, we are unable to enjoy the fact that winning is still winning.

I gave this some thought as I embarked on my writing career. I had no idea if I would attract a readership and if I did, how my books would be received. Ultimately, I wondered, would my words have meaning and would my story lines and characters resonate? And what if I only sold a handful of books instead of thousands: would I be happy with that? Could I find fulfillment if positive reviews and accolades failed to materialize? And if the New York Times never came to call would I be satisfied? I gave some thought to these questions and others before I began. And in the end, my personal response freed me, giving me permission to attack my dreams with gusto, regardless of the outcome. I wanted to write because it brought me joy, fulfilling my need to create. I hoped to produce something to leave behind for generations who were yet to be born, those who might never know me. I had always thought that someday I would do this, and in retirement, I finally had the time to do it. Removing the pressure to succeed made me successful. Being diagnosed with cancer gave me a sense of urgency.

And so, I encourage you to be kind to yourself as you embark on a project, big or small. Paint a room or even one wall instead of the whole house. Take photos for your social media pages and frame the best ones. Plant a few flowers. Celebrate the small victories. They are much bigger than you might think.

Who knows? You might just surprise yourself!

My Magical Month

I wrote this the year before I was diagnosed. That was when my symptoms first appeared, when I was far too busy to pay much attention to them. But it is one of my most precious memories, one I wanted to share. Fall always reminds me of "my magical month."

I have been trying to pen this for three days now, but I have an excuse for my distraction. I currently live with a four-year-old. Well, his parents live here, too, through a recent twist of fate, the Louisiana flood, which landed them back home for a few weeks as they relocate. As he so simply describes it, "the river came and took all of my toys, but it's OK." He is resilient, which is only one of his many charms. So for now, ours is a three generational home. But that's not the story here. He is.

I haven't been around a young one so consistently since my own children were that age. My other grandchildren are older (and more worldly, of course), so I am having such fun with this one. And I have once again been immersed into that magical world of wonderment, where life is filled with giggles and big wet kisses. It is snakes and snails and puppy dog tails around here, and it is pretty darned special.

I have watched with fascination as he has rearranged the patio, his careful construction of chairs and sprinklers and empty pots and random bits of cardboard resulting in elaborate tableaus, which serve a purpose. One, he has labeled a "bee catcher;" another is a "grasshopper playground." I marvel at his designs, the engineering both intricate and intriguing. But I am also inspired by his imagination, his never-waning spirit of fun and adventure. We have taken walks to the lake, where we built a "sand" castle, mostly made of mud, and took to the woods, collecting pine cones to put in a bowl as a nod to autumn. We are sharing moments, making memories.

Last night, he fell on the floor as he launched into his best android routine. Apparently, it is something he does with regularity, a routine performance, but staged just for me. His stiffened movements, carefully choreographed, did make him seem rather mechanical and robotic; his one-liners, silly catchphrases, added to the affect. It was cute. I was instructed to press the imaginary reset button on his back and the other on his nose and then much to my delight, watched him spring into action, returning, like a modern day Pinocchio, into a real boy. It is hard to conceal my amusement over his antics.

As soon as he wakes in the morning, he is searching for me, squealing with delight as he announces, "found you." I am greeted by a toothy grin, followed by a bear hug. It is one of those lovely life moments that never fails to thrill me. And when he is gone, I will miss it. You see, in his world, I am special, the one who secretly passes him cookies before dinner and never tells him "no." It is a grandparent privilege earned from raising my own children to responsible adulthood.

Like me, he is talkative: his constant chatter, both engaging and insightful. His speech is punctuated by "OK?" to show his need for understanding and "Come on: are you kidding me?" as he gestures wildly over something he finds hard to believe. I found myself using those same words yesterday, his influence on me far greater than mine on him.

He loves the doggies, lavishing them with attention. And even the old one, our blind canine curmudgeon, who bites anybody who gets too close, has fallen under his spell, allowing himself to be poked and prodded with a patience we rarely get to see. Today, he proudly pronounced that when he grows us up he is going to be a "vet doctor." He will be a good one.

There is something enchanting about children, the way they view the world and their place in it. They lack the cynicism that comes with growing up. And I am ever so grateful for this concentrated bit of time with my youngest grandson, who has enriched my life in ways I never could have imagined. Ironically, I wrote last week about leaving something behind, particularly in reference to my writing. But as I spend time with this precious little boy, I am reminded that a true legacy isn't in anything tangible: it is in the children who carry your genes and share your history. It is in the memories you make with those who are part of your very soul. I could write more, of course, but he is waiting for me. He wants to play. And right now, that is my priority.

Excuse my Absence

It is almost Halloween. Ghouls and goblins and pumpkins are readily available for purchase in the stores. Oh, and ghosts, of course. I have always thought of ghost as a noun. *She thought she saw a ghost.* Or an adjective. *He loved to tell ghost stories.* But recently, it has made its way into the urban dictionary as a verb. *I thought we were friends, but she ghosted me.* It means to suddenly disappear. And I guess I did that with this blog. Gee, I am sorry.

When I finished the last post to be included in *Still Ovacoming,* I thought I would take a short break. Treatment had been difficult and a bad case of chemo brain made writing coherently a real challenge. Besides, I imagined, folks had to be getting tired of reading about cancer. No matter how positively I tried to spin it, the fact that I am fighting a potentially terminal disease remains true. Even the most devoted Pollyanna might find it hard to see something uplifting in that, I figured.

But I was wrong.

I forgot about the folks who read these blog posts. I got texts and emails and cards from people who were concerned when there were no updates. I didn't realize how much people cared. And that meant something to me. So let me fill you in on what has happened in the past five weeks: I finished treatment. Those are three of the sweetest words ever spoken besides "I love you," of course. The final day was a long one, but my dear friend and talented photographer tagged along to document the moment. We laughed and cried as she snapped pictures, which now remind me of what I have endured. The incredible staff at the infusion center made my parting moment special as I rang the bell signifying the end. And from what I understand they went to great lengths to make that happen since it wasn't standard operating procedure. I was surrounded by such kindness and affection that day, which filled my heart with joyful hope.

Two weeks later, I had an early-morning PET scan to see how well it all worked. I have already written about the process, which is always daunting. This time, I got to visit the new imaging center, which meant state of the art equipment and shorter time spent in the tube. And then, I waited.

The next day, the call came. My doctor's nurse was singing, "Celebrate good times." I began to cry as my body went limp with relief. The report stated, "total and complete response to surgery and treatment with no evidence of disease." I am cancer free.

Praise the Lord.

I am not going to lie; my body is still struggling to recover from the potent doses of poison. I am tired most days, even if those are spent doing little to nothing. My sense of taste is slowly returning. And yes, I am still completely bald. I look forward to growing some lashes and brows. I long to look and feel like myself again.

But I am grateful…. So grateful…. God has been good to me, healed my broken body twice and kept me safe through the grueling process of recovery. I often question what I have done to deserve His grace and mercy, but there are no real answers because fortunately, I couldn't have earned it even if tried. That's the beauty of His unconditional love.

I thank you all for the prayers. This is our miracle and a testament of what happens when two or more gather together. There is great power in collective faith. I know that much is true.

So what's next? I am to go on a PARP inhibitor, which is classified as a chemo pill. Big pharma thinks it is worth $34,000 a month. My insurance company isn't quite sure of that. And so I wait while they battle it out. Stay tuned. That should make for some interesting observations.

The Prescription

The call came before I had poured my first cup of coffee, but I promptly answered since I had been waiting for it for several weeks. The voice on the other end of the line was polite and professional. I laughed nervously as we exchanged pleasantries. She was from the specialty pharmacy, and she had my fate in her hands.

You see, the last time I completed chemo, I had gleefully celebrated my remission status. I firmly believed that I was done, finished, cured. I naively thought that my biggest challenge in the months and years ahead would be growing hair and losing the steroid weight. I was wrong. So this time, when my doctor suggested a maintenance drug, a parp inhibitor that offered the possibility of keeping the beast from returning, I readily agreed to try it.

The oncology nurse had carefully reviewed the long list of side effects with me. I was asked to sign an acknowledgment that I understood the risks. But as I have learned in this life, rewards must be weighed against those risks, and having a chance to stay cancer free is worth it to me. Besides, I figured, as long as I didn't grow a beard or a tail, as long as my ears didn't fall off, I would handle it.

I had already been forewarned that it would take a few weeks for the paperwork to be processed and submitted to insurance because it was a pricey drug. I took a deep breath before asking the question. Sometimes, curiosity isn't a good thing. Just ask Pandora.

"How much IS it?" I asked.

"Twelve thousand a month for your dosage."

"I'm sorry," I said, "I thought you said 'twelve grand.'"

"I did. And yes, I know. It was hard for me to believe, too."

Even without a calculator I was able to do the quick multiplication. I had been prescribed a potentially life-saving drug which cost $144,000 a year. My mind raced over the implications, the scenarios of all the things I might buy with that kind of money. A small house? A luxury car or two? An around-the-world vacation, first class? I thought of the good I would be able to do with that amount of cash. How many hungry children could I feed? How many college scholarships could I give away? Of course, it was all a bit of fantasy because such a sum was pie-in-the sky unrealistic for me. And this drug might also be out of reach financially, I quickly realized.

I began to speculate about copays. If my insurance agreed to approve it and bore the majority of the cost, it could still be exorbitant. Even at ten percent, it would cost $3400 a month, or $40,800 annually. I tried not to laugh out loud at the absurdity of that number.

I did some research and discovered that because of a complicated qualification system, I wasn't eligible for assistance from the drug manufacturer, nor could I realistically use any coupons or discounts. I also learned that many women, even those with decent coverage, have a difficult time paying for it because of its exorbitant price. This, along with inflated hospital costs, is why insurance premiums have skyrocketed, making the cost of medical care prohibitive. It is disconcerting, for all of us.

Let's face it: so much of battling this disease is out of my control, which often makes me feel helpless. I hate that part most of all. I tried not to worry, which was easier said than done.

I stumbled across an article this week based on an interview with the CEO of a major pharmaceutical company. His corporation had been buying the expired patents of many common drugs and selling them on a proprietary basis for five hundred times what they had been just a few years ago. Meanwhile, the new drugs, based on breakthrough research, are being marketed and sold at record- breaking prices. And as a result, the patients struggle to afford them, especially those who are underinsured or uninsured. When asked if he felt a moral obligation to people who were ill, his reply was ruthless, but straightforward. "I am in the business of making money for stockholders, not to heal anyone," he said. Quite frankly, by the time I had finished reading the article I felt a little sick myself.

I know that cancer is big business. My course of chemotherapy this time cost well over $500,000. And that was for six triple infusions, the accompanying medication, and regular bloodwork. I certainly didn't pay half a million out of pocket, but these two years of fighting the disease has taken its financial toll, even with good insurance. Now, this new phase of treatment also comes with a hefty price tag.

And so, I had nervously waited the four weeks for that phone call.

"What is my copay?" I asked almost immediately.

"We will get to that at the end of the interview," she said, her voice practiced and courteous.

"You should tell me that now in case there is no need for an interview," I said.

"Let's see," she said, pausing to look for the information. I held my breath. "Your part will be $84.50 per month."

I exhaled, then asked her to repeat it, which she did. I began to cry with relief, loudly wailing into the phone. "I'm so grateful," I mumbled between sobs, unable to say much more.

And for a moment there was a crack in her serious demeanor as she whispered, "I am happy it worked out for you. You have made my day."

This time, I am one of the lucky ones, and I know it. Some are not as fortunate, which makes me sad. And I am ever so thankful to be given a chance to fight this beast with the newest drug available.

God is good. Always.

And yes, I'll let you know if I grow a tail.

The Language Lesson

Just for the heck of it, I figure it might be a good idea to switch gears and post about something not cancer-related. So in honor of the beginning of a new school year, I thought I would share one of my favorite memories of when I was in the classroom.

It was the first day of a new school year, and I eagerly greeted my students. Instead of the usual roll call, I suggested self-introductions. After all, it was a course in communication, heavy on building interpersonal skills, with public speaking thrown in for good measure. One-by-one, the students tentatively gave their names, along with a bit of information about themselves.

I saw the panic in her eyes as it got close to her turn. She was tiny, shy and, obviously, not American-born. "I not speak English," she said hesitantly. My mind raced. Was she is in the wrong class? I smiled reassuringly as made my way over to check her schedule. But she was indeed where she was supposed to be, with a very Asian first and last name that, ironically, I was unable to pronounce. I nodded. Nonverbal language was universal, I figured. I pointed to her name and looked at her questioningly. She said it softly and then paused as though frantically searching for the words. Finally, she added, "I new here." There was a stillness in the room, and then, the class cheered. And from that moment on, I knew that we were all about to embark on a very special journey together.

I watched with pride as the days turned into weeks, then months, as my high school students took turns engaging her in casual conversation, instructing her on how to respond to their questions. They asked about her culture, life in Korea with genuine interest. I noticed that they mentored her through assignments and made her practice in before-school tutoring sessions They encouraged her when her turn came to take to the podium to address the group, prompting her when she hesitated for the right word. And they delighted in her triumphs as she worked tirelessly to demystify the complicated nuances of the English language. Each day, her speaking skills grew as her vocabulary expanded. Of course, I had to resist the overwhelming urge to help, to simplify, to slip into instructor/mother hen mode as her teacher. But my students subtly let me know that they had her peer education well in hand, and they most certainly did. It warmed my heart.

As we approached the end of the semester, the last big challenge loomed large for all of them, a policy debate. Not only did it require analysis of research material, but it also entailed constructing an elaborate brief, synthesis of ideas and on-your-feet refutation of the opponent's argument. Could she do it? We all waited in breathless anticipation as she addressed the group, notes in hand.

"Resolved: that the SAT should be abolished for admission into public colleges and universities," she announced in her pronounced accent. We collectively held our breath. And as she slowly presented her side, built a case, and answered the opposition's questions, we slowly exhaled. She was brilliant! And when the winner was announced, she beamed with pride as she claimed her prize, a plastic trophy I had bought from the dollar store.

But the reality was they were all winners, as they experienced the joy of helping another human being reach her full potential. Yes, it was amazing to watch the magic that group of kids created. But the most powerful lesson to come out of my classroom that year is that kindness is indeed a universal language. And the most grateful student was this teacher.

Saying Goodbye to Boudreaux

It has taken me a couple of days to process the fact that he is indeed gone, that sixteen in dog years is more like a century to humans and that his poor little body just deteriorated, obliterating his puppy spirit in the process. I watched and waited, hoping for a sign that it was time, that I hadn't selfishly prolonged his life just to have him in mine. And as he has for so very long, he let me know what he wanted. And with a heavy heart, I obliged him.

His death was peaceful thanks to the loving care of a mobile vet, a friend of my daughter-in-law, who came immediately. We sat on the kitchen floor, and I held him, wrapped in his favorite blanket as I offered him a slice of bologna, his favorite, which he surprisingly ate with gusto. And he didn't flinch at the injection as he just drifted off to sleep, his breathing slowed until it was no more. As I kissed him goodbye, thanking him for so many years of love and companionship, I knew that I had done the right thing for him, having eased his suffering and pain. It was the last gift I could give him.

And so, I have spent the moments which have followed, thinking back on his life, his days upon this planet. I am often reminded that because dogs are with us for a brief time, they must pack a lot in their shortened lifetime. And he did. He was tiny when I got him, a little ball of fur, who could fit into the palm of my hand. The day after he became mine, I sneaked him off to school on a staff development day, and he quietly slept in my lap as I sat through one boring faculty meeting after another, a memory that has remained with me after all this time. As the runt of the litter, he somehow grew a heart that was a little bigger, a little braver. He would set off in the woods, exploring with wild abandon, completely unaware that he was small, compared to many of the critters that lurked on our property. Because he was a foo foo white dog, he often returned home covered in mud, dragging sticks behind him, a look of guilt on his dirty face, hating the bath which followed, the price he paid for his wild adventures. He could run faster than a four wheeler and knew all the shortcuts, taking great delight in the race, beating the rider in the family to his destination. Proudly, he would stand on the front porch, surveying the land, his protective instinct piqued, and I often worried that he would tie into something he couldn't handle, thinking he was saving us. But in spite of his bold spirit, at the end of the day, he was simply my fur baby, who cuddled with me, sighing with contentment as he drifted off to sleep.

I will miss his greeting when I return home, whether it was an absence of ten minutes or ten days. He never failed to make me feel that I was most important in his world. And on difficult days, when people and circumstances were disappointing for me, he was there to comfort me, to assure me that tomorrow would come, washing away the pain of today.

There are lovely platitudes, which pay homage to the loving nature of a dog. And I could quote many of them here, because they are true. Instead, I will simply say that I have always thought that dogs find the people who need them, when the time is right, often filling a void a person didn't even know they had. Boudreaux did that for me. They come into our lives, teaching us about love and loyalty and trust. And when they depart, they teach us about grief and loss, the toll exacted for that love. There is something about a great dog that stays with us forever. And that is part of their magic as they leave behind quite a legacy.

The Mystery Cat

The package of hamburger buns had been ripped open with two partially eaten. Crumbs were scattered all over the kitchen counter and onto the floor. Only two of us live in this house. I knew that I certainly hadn't made the mess. I sighed as I went in search of my husband.

"Did you get hungry in the middle of the night?" I asked, trying to disguise my annoyance.

"No. Why?"

"It seems that somebody was in a hurry to get into the buns last night and didn't bother to clean up the crime scene. Wasn't me. Had to be you."

He shook his head. "Nope. Can't confess to something I didn't do."

I shrugged and returned to the kitchen. The scullery maid duties usually fall to me. I retrieved the broom and dust pan from the pantry.

"Must have been the cat," he called from the other room.

I stopped in my tracks. He was trying to be funny. "We don't have a cat," I said, tossing the entire bag of now-stale bread into the garbage.

"We had one in here yesterday morning. It was hanging out in the living room, perched on the curtain rod."

I paused to consider what he has said. "Seriously? And what did you do?"

"Went to get some coffee. By the time I got back, it was gone."

"Gone where?" I was beginning to feel like I had fallen into a bad game of twenty questions.

"Outside, I guess."

"Did you try to shoo it out?"

"No. Just figured it would leave the same way it came in."

I took a deep breath and closed my eyes, hoping to channel my inner Namaste before I lost my temper. "Keep calm," I whispered to myself.

We may or may not have a cat on the loose in our house, I thought. But where had it come from? I have three neighbors. I called them, asking if anyone had a missing pet. Nope. None of them even had a cat either. We live in the middle of nowhere. It must have been feral, I guessed. That could make the situation even more complicated. Just my luck.

My mind raced with possibilities. The weather had recently turned cool after a long, hot summer. We eagerly opened the doors, welcoming the crisp fall air into a house that had been closed tight for months. I guess the kitty thought it to be a sign that it was welcomed.

Now what, I wondered?

And so I waited. Later that afternoon, my husband spotted it again, casually strolling through the back hall like it owned the place. He came to get me, but by the time we had both returned, it was gone. Wasn't that convenient, I thought? I was starting to suspect that perhaps I was the object of some silly joke. Candid Camera hadn't been on TV for a long time, I rationalized. But isn't October a time ripe for pranks, especially one that involves a ghostly cat? I reminded myself that it is best to keep a sense of humor at such moments.

I was, nevertheless, a little frantic just thinking about the potential consequences. An undomesticated cat could wreak havoc in my house. We had to find it. My husband went in search of the live trap, one we had once used to catch squirrels in the attic. I prepared the bait, a fresh can of tuna. We placed it in the middle of the den, adjacent to the kitchen. If it had found food here once, it would most likely return when hungry.

The next morning, the trap rested there, empty, but the kitchen garbage can had been upturned., and there was a vile smell permeating the house. My sensitive nose led me to the basement room. It was a disaster. Two lamps had been knocked off of tables. A picture had fallen off the wall. A decorative plate and vase were shattered. The bracket holding a surround sound speaker, which hung by two thin wires, was in pieces. And to add insult to injury, there, in the middle of the sofa, was a disgusting pile of poop. This explained the awful odor.

My stomach churned in protest.

I got to work cleaning up the mess and disinfecting everything in sight. I cursed under my breath as my husband set up a second live trap.

Let's face it: even the most astute detective sometimes fails to solve a crime. Even the most experienced hunter sometimes fails to bag the prized trophy. And sometimes, even smarty pants people are outsmarted. This is one of those times. But by a cat? Gee.

It has been four days. And no, we still have not caught it yet. Heck, I still haven't even seen it. Our dog, Lola, is no help, oblivious to its intruding presence as she naps comfortably on the sofa. Meanwhile, I am trying to think like a cat, going through lots of bait and sleeping with one eye open.

I am reminded of TS Eliot's poem, "Macavity, the Mystery Cat." In his honor, I have given this feline the same name, for it, too, is a master criminal, who has broken every human law. And like Eliot's hero, it's useless to investigate because

"You seek him in the basement, you may look up in the air.

But I tell you once and once again, Macavity's not there."

So I will end here and keep you all posted. You see, I need to go to the store to stock up on tuna. I hear that Kroger is running a sale. And maybe, while I am there, I ought to invest in a litter box, just for good measure. It couldn't hurt.

The Cat, Part II

The electric opener made quick work of the canned fish. I carefully drained the water and emptied the contents into a small bowl. Without thinking much about it, I added the chopped eggs, mayonnaise, pickles, and a dash of mustard while the bread toasted. For the second time this week, I was having a tuna sandwich for lunch. I glanced at the inventory in the pantry. I had bought far too much for a phantom feline that either had no fondness for it or was off on an adventure elsewhere. Somebody had to eat it, and that somebody was me.

My friends have asked about the mysterious cat. Let's face it: everyone wants a story to have an ending, preferably a happy one. This one has neither. I have spent the past ten days searching for the elusive kitty, examining every cupboard and closet for a sign. I have inspected every nook and cranny of the attic, basement, and garage. I have set out bowls of food and milk, the best bait I could find, but they remain untouched. The only sign that he has been around is some mighty interesting patterns in the garden mulch. Perhaps he views that as one big litter box. But the areas I have recently raked smooth remain so. He has either been raptured to heaven or moved on to greener pastures, although I can imagine neither as a plausible scenario. Regardless, he is gone.

I would lie if I said I missed him. I never even saw him, and except for the messes he made during his initial visit, he could have been an apparition, a figment of the imagination. I guess I will never know.

It has been said that one does not adopt a cat; rather, a cat adopts you. Some have gone so far to say that a feline will find its destined family and claim them as its own. If that is true, then, I guess we failed as a prospective home. Perhaps my ego is bruised a little, but my mind tells me that I dodged a furry little bullet. However, as the crisp days of autumn are soon to be replaced by winter's chill, I can't help but wonder if we will see him again. Maybe I will keep a can or two of this tuna just in case.

Saving Things for Good

We ate dinner last night on the fancy china, and we used the good silver. It wasn't a special celebration. The menu wasn't anything out of the ordinary, since meatloaf is rarely noted as fancy food, but somehow, it felt festive. But it was also significant.

You see, I was raised by parents who grew up during the Depression Era, which somehow made them more in tune to the intrinsic value of things. They recycled and reused before it was the environmentally conscientious thing to do. And they saved for what they wanted, rather than buying on credit. Their frugality used to bother me, especially when they used the all-too-familiar motto, "save it for good." They believed that you should use or wear the old stuff on a regular basis, with the nicer things reserved for some sacred moment, worthy of the occasion.

I never understood the reasoning behind it, especially when it interfered with my plans. I once had a pair of petal pink patent leather shoes. (My obsession with shoes started when I was quite young, it seems.) Oh, how I longed for them! When my mom finally agreed that I could have them for Easter, I was thrilled. I wore them to church, along with my beribboned bonnet, and when Monday morning rolled around, I slipped them on to wear to school, anxious to show my friends. But Mom was firm in her refusal, handing me my scuffed loafers instead. "Those," she said, pointing to the objects of my affection, "are to be kept for good." And ironically, as a growing girl, whose feet expanded exponentially, within six Sundays they were painfully tight and handed down to some other little girl in pristine condition.

It's funny how we become programmed by those childhood lessons. And instead of rejecting the idea, I embraced it as I grew older. I kept the pricey scented candles on display, but never lit them. Eventually, they simply smelled like wax. I used the stained and faded dishtowels, keeping the nice ones for when company came. They were practically unusable from dry rot when I took them out at dinner parties. I cooked with the old pots, reserving the nice shiny ones for holidays. There are other examples, of course, from sexy underwear to fine wine, but quite frankly, it is far too embarrassing to list them.

I am pleased to say that this all changed for me one day when I bought my granddaughter a fancy little party dress. She was delighted, her eyes sparkling as she ran her fingers across its lacy bodice. So when we got home from the store, and she rushed to put it on to play in, I was aghast. I took a deep breath and then launched into a lecture about how lovely it will be to have that dress to wear for some exciting event and why "saving it for good" would serve her well. She wanted to please me, but I saw the disappointment on her face, and I remembered how I simply wanted to sport those pink shoes when I was her age. How could I deny something that brought her such joy? I smiled and told her that she should wear it for the rest of the day. I watched with delight as she happily twirled around the kitchen. Later on, we went out for ice cream. A pretty dress can make any given Tuesday a "for good" moment.

Would you Like Some Cheese with that Whine?

I was eight years old, visiting my grandma, who answered the door with several band aid strips strategically placed on her face. I thought that she had been terribly injured until she smiled broadly and welcomed me inside. My curiosity was piqued, of course, but since I had been taught to respect my elders, I waited for what I thought was an appropriate amount of time before I asked the obvious question.

"It is helping me get rid of wrinkles," she simply said, as though it was the most natural thing in the world, that the secret to defying gravity rested in that red, white, and blue box.

My young brain couldn't figure out how it did so, but I took her at her word. And to this day, I can't look at a box of bandages without wondering if I should give it a try, especially now since the combination of age and sun and chemo have had their way with me.

Momma always watched her weight, careful not to "let herself go" as she liked to call it. Most of the female members of my family colored their hair and had perfected the application of natural-looking makeup. Southern women tend to be schooled in the womanly art of good grooming from the time they are little girls. It is part of our DNA, and attempting to look as attractive as possible is as natural to us as breathing. So is it any wonder, then, that I am a little upset that cancer has completely changed the way I see myself?

Yeah, I am so vain, I probably think this chapter is about me. It is. (My apologies to Carly Simon. and my readers. This is pretty self-indulgent, and I know it.)

It has been two months since I had my last dose of chemo poison. That's sixty days. And by now, I had fully expected to look in the mirror and recognize the person whose image is reflected back at me. I figured that with the steroids out of my system, the weight would have magically fallen off my body, and I would have a grand time rediscovering the treasures in my closet. Nothing makes you feel worse than not being able to squeeze into your favorite jeans. That's one of those universal truths. And by the way, it's why Wonder Woman wears tights.

But the needle on the scale hasn't budged one bit, in spite of better eating habits and more exercise than when I was in treatment. Getting dressed to go anywhere is a challenge, as the casualties mount on my bed, each item tossed aside and rejected. I fully expected to be done with this by now, the bloat subsiding and my former self emerging like those butterflies I love so much. It hasn't happened.

But that's not all. Except for the three wiry whiskers on my chin, I am still completely hairless. My bald head glistens in the light, and with the cooler fall temperatures setting in, I find myself shivering as I scramble for a soft cap to wear. I have an assortment of wigs, of course, and they have helped me look and feel less like a cancer patient, but hanging around the house in a wig seems silly to me, not to mention downright uncomfortable, so I get to see more of my baldness than I would like. And then, there is the lack of brows and lashes. My morning routine begins with a careful inspection of my eyes and the expectation that hair has miraculously started to grow during the night. I try not to be disappointed as I draw on my features, hoping to look less like a cartoon character and more like myself.

Compared to last time, I am behind schedule with this. It could be the chemo pill, I am told. I admit to being terribly impatient. But then, I had the grand epiphany that worrying about growing hair beats worrying about dying. If I end up permanently bald, it is the price I will have paid for this time of recovery. I hope that I can embrace the possibility of an altered appearance in exchange for being where I currently am. Perception always changes with experience, right?

My husband calls me Ned (for "no evidence of disease"). It conveniently rhymes with bald head and said, thread, bed, ahead…Well, you get the point. I am reminded that it also couples with dead, and I am most certainly alive. Thank God. Perhaps worrying about how I look is simply a reminder that I am human that I am responsive to life again, and that I am still attached to this shell which houses my soul.

In spite of my shallow obsessions, I try to remember to be grateful, whispering prayers of thanksgiving throughout the day. Truly, I am blessed to be in remission once more. But if you know of any good potions for hair growth, pass them along. I am always optimistic about tomorrow. It is a good way to live.

Kindness Matters

―――――❦―――――

Two years ago today, I was wheeled into an operating room for debulking surgery. For those unfamiliar with the term, it means removing as much of the cancerous tissue and tumor as possible. I needed nine weeks of chemotherapy before my doctor would even attempt mine. I tend to do things on a grand scale, even cancer. I will spare you the details, but when they finished, I was pretty much like a fishbowl in the abdominal area. It is an interesting bit of imagery, right? But that's not the point here. It is an anniversary, one of many that has come with this disease. I tend to commemorate them all because doing so is a chance to celebrate life. But it is also a chance to be introspective, to think about how far I have come as I have walked this path.

Mercifully, I have outlived my original prognosis, the projected limits placed upon my existence. And I have learned some remarkable truths as well as I try to respond to live rather than react to it. Now, as I stare at a blank computer screen, I wonder if I have any more profound words of wisdom to share. Or do I think that all of my ideas have been used up, that anything I write now is redundant and repetitive? I wait for my muse to make an appearance. Sometimes, she is missing in action for long periods of time. Fickle girl.

But then, the doorbell rings, interrupting my concentration. It is the mail carrier with a big heavy box addressed to me. I open it and find that the inside of the box has been decorated with bright yellow paper with the words "A box full of sunshine to brighten your day." Inside, there are yellow treats of every description, and I am like a kid on Christmas morning exploring it all, thrilled beyond words.

My heart is full of love and appreciation. You see, kindness changes things, including people. I suppose that the past two and a half years have made me aware of just how many friendly, generous, and considerate people there are in this world. I have been blessed to have been cared for by some incredibly compassionate folks and have a medical team whose warmth and concern has been as integral a part of my healing as the drugs that they dispense. I've had friends who have gone out of their way to keep my spirits up, visiting with me when I was lonely or sitting with me for long hours while I received chemo. I've had homemade soup and good books delivered to my door. My closest pals have endured hours of listening to me wallow in the self-pity, and then, patiently whisked me off for a bit of retail therapy afterwards. Yes, indeed, I have been the recipient of overwhelming kindness. And I am thankful for it.

We have been told that the fittest survive, which we tend to associate with selfishness. Society paints us with a broad brush as biologically competitive and self-indulgent. But for the most part, I have not found that to be true. I think that empathy and caring for others is a part of our DNA, that the desire to be helpful is instinctual. Witness how tenderly young children treat animals and each other, and you will see that blatant self-regard is a learned behavior, not an innate one. Noticing those around us who are suffering, celebrating another's successes, or helping ease someone's burden certainly makes the world a better place. But it has a personal impact as well, the boomerang effect. In fact, giving to others can often be a source of satisfaction and fulfillment. It absolutely enhances relationships and lubricates the workplace.

Today, I am certainly grateful to be the recipient of this thoughtful surprise package, which boosted my morale in countless ways. I read the enclosed card with tears in my eyes. The gift was from a former student, one whom I had taught many, many years ago. How lovely to be remembered, I thought. And then, I read the last line. "Don't ever stop writing your blog. You continue to teach us through your words."

Ah, that fickle muse of mine. She is often late, but today, she was right on time.

The Party

It has been a while since I have had a get-together of my own like that. The reasons are pretty obvious, but I guess having people over is among the many things I miss about my pre-cancer life. It is fun to play Martha Stewart on occasion, to drag out the seldom-used china and serving platters, and cook up those favorite dishes. Let's face it: nothing brings people together like a good party.

I am going to a holiday party given by one of my best friends. I am looking forward to it. The woman knows how to make folks feel at home in her home. She is a relaxed hostess with a generous spirit, so it will be a fun time. The food will be great, and I look forward to seeing mutual friends. 'Tis the season, right?

It has been a while since I have had a get-together of my own like that. The reasons are pretty obvious, but I guess having people over is among the many things I miss about my pre-cancer life. It is fun to play Martha Stewart on occasion, to drag out the seldom-used china and serving platters, and cook up those favorite dishes. Let's face it: nothing brings people together like a good party.

Except maybe a funeral.

Hold on. I am not taking a morbid detour here. Where I am from, home of the jazz processions and massive above-ground tombs, attendees often dance their way to the graveyard. There is usually a big soiree afterwards. The tables are laden with every kind of dish imaginable, while the beer and wine flow freely. The room quickly fills with the sounds of merriment as people tell story after story about the life of the deceased. Some seem like tall tales, exaggerated for effect, but the purpose is to celebrate a life well-lived and a person well-loved. Yes, it is quite the spectacle, but somehow, it makes the grief bearable. Laughter and tears, like joy and grief, are opposite emotions, but equally strong reactions. It is okay to feel both at such times.

Sadly, the dearly departed never gets to hear the carefully-practiced eulogy or see who shows up to pay their respects. Nope, a dead person is unable to attend the big tribute held in his honor or taste the chicken casserole made by Cousin Sue. What a shame.

I am reminded of Tom Sawyer, who, in Twain's novel, fakes his death and then, secretly attends his own funeral. He listens with rapt attention to the speakers, who shower him with praise, later remarking that it was "the proudest moment of my life." Isn't peeking into life after one is gone to see just how much we are missed one of the great fantasies? Sometimes I think that life should imitate art.

So here is a thought: what about a "living funeral" for someone who is very old or very ill? (And yes, that term is indeed an oxymoron.) But it isn't such a bad idea, is it? I think being able to say goodbye, while being surrounded by those whose lives have been aligned with ours in big and small ways would be pretty wonderful. Being part of the celebration, rather than the object of it, might be interesting and enjoyable. In other words, why wait until someone is gone to honor them, to let them know their life has made a difference in yours? And it's the perfect reason to have a party!

I am not much of a country music fan, but Tanya Tucker just released a new song, "Bring my Flowers Now," which perfectly expresses this powerful message. (Ask Mr. Google to play it for you. It really is beautiful.) Spend time with those who mean something to you while you can; tell them how important they are while they are able to hear the words. Enjoy being in the company of those you love. This moment is all any of us are guaranteed, so embrace it and each other.

My bestie brought me two dozen roses this week. Yeah, she gets it without even hearing the song. I told you that she is special.

And no, I am not planning my own goodbye celebration anytime soon, but maybe I will have a Mardi Gras party in a few months. I have some beads in the attic. I can still make a mean gumbo, too. We will act a little crazy and get a little loud. I'll buy flowers. There are some folks to whom I certainly owe big fragrant bouquets. Sooner than later.

To Rest

I can't take credit for this. It originated with God, first book, Old Testament. How many times have we read the story of creation, how the Almighty formed the earth with His very own hands, shaped the creatures of the land, sky and sea before finally, making man? Indeed, within the first few chapters, we are given some pretty important lessons about how we are expected to live. And not all of them relate to that darned apple.

I have been listening to a Biblical podcast recommended to me by one of my medical team. The scholars dissect the meaning behind those familiar passages, and I admittedly find their take on things fascinating. But it has also given me some of food for my own thought. And, of course, that means I need to share.

The story of that first week, when our earthly domain was established, culminates in day seven, when God rested. I can remember as a child thinking that making a world must have been exhausting for Our Lord. What else would explain His need to prop up His feet and chill when He was done? Of course, now, I understand that He was modeling something for us rather than taking care of Himself. He was showing us that it is perfectly fine and even holy to do the same.

So much of our identity as a human being is connected to what we do for a living, what education we have earned, and what accolades we have won. We ask strangers about their hobbies, and respond with admiration for the marathon runners and creative artists. Such questioning is a regular part of the informal interviews that we conduct when we meet folks, and often, our perception of others is tied to the answers. We respect success and honor a strong work ethic. But perhaps more importantly, such ideas affect the way we view ourselves. We begin the inevitable judgment, which often leaves us feeling that we have somehow fallen short, by comparison. That's unfortunate. And unfair. And wrong.

Most cultures tend to value busyness. We are blatantly told, in fact, that being idle is bad. Do a quick internet search and you will find quotes from philosophers to kings about the evils of doing nothing. It leads to all manner of wickedness, they say, since obviously nothing good can possibly come from doing nothing.

But on the seventh day, God rested, right?

Having cancer can be exhausting. For me, one of the most difficult parts of being sick has been the overwhelming fatigue. It is not a normal tired, like at the end of a long day of work or exercise. No, it is worse, much worse. Walking to the kitchen to get a drink of water often feels like climbing Mt. Everest.

Your arms and legs feel heavy and disconnected from the rest of your body. Everything feels like a chore. And while the cancer brochures admonish that staying active is best, somehow just the idea of it is completely draining.

And so, I rest.

It has taken me a long time to give myself permission to spend a day in bed, watching mindless TV or flipping through one internet source after another. I had to work through the guilt of not being able to cook or do laundry like I once did. And learning how to ignore the dust bunnies and cobwebs has been a process. I am not idle, I tell myself, not building some workshop for the devil. I am healing, trying hard to repair my broken body. And that is good.

Allowing myself to "simply be" has encouraged me to think in ways I never have before. Sometimes a relaxed mind becomes fertile ground for self-discovery. That's been an added benefit. Even for the able-bodied, being still in this land of abundant noise and rampant chaos, can be physically and spiritually therapeutic. We worry and fret and labor all week long only to tackle another kind of to-do list on our days off. Certainly, this can't be healthy for the body or good for the soul.

It is perfectly fine to stop the world for a moment, exhale, and just relax. In fact, it is highly recommended. Just ask God. And He wrote it all down for us, just in case we forget.

The Thankful Book

Most of us are familiar with the phrase "sleep like a baby." How we long for that kind of blissful, uninterrupted rest. Let's face it: the further we get from those early moments of infancy, the more challenging sleep becomes. By the time we reach adulthood, we regularly wake through the night, mentally reviewing a to-do list or worrying about the "what ifs" in life. It is a nocturnal ritual that so many of us recreate more often than not. I am no exception.

Lately, however, I am roused, not by anxiety, but with gratitude. In the still of the night, I am reminded that I am very much alive, hopeful and optimistic about my tomorrows. I have learned to chase moments with reverent thanksgiving, giving up much of the griping and complaining that I often used to express. It is a huge shift in perception for me, an improvement in the way I view the world.

Illness has somehow cracked open the bubble of superficiality that I once lived in and allowed me to see more clearly. I don't have the time, nor do I want to spend the energy, fretting about the shallow stuff, which most of it is, by the way. Instead, I understand that every breath is a miracle and every day is an opportunity. This shift in thinking hasn't come easy, but it has been life-changing.

A few months ago, a friend sent me a lovely book, which focuses on the holy practice pf being thankful, especially for the small, often noticed, things. And while its theme is nothing new, the accompanying challenge to write down every single instance of gratitude was something I had never even considered beyond my failed attempts to journal daily. Because the author presents a beautifully written and compelling argument. I was intrigued with the idea, inspired to give it a try. By the time I had finished reading the last chapter, I had a new notebook and my favorite pen at the ready to capture my fleeting thoughts during the day.

I began with the big things, of course: my faith, which comforts me; my precious family and devoted friends, who support me; my home, which is my safe place; the medical team, who work so tirelessly on my behalf. I glanced over at my old dog, sleeping just inches from where I sat. Certainly, I was grateful for her faithful companionship. Then, I expanded the list with preferred foods, beloved books, and favorite songs. My mind raced with memories of the sun on my bare shoulders and the cool breeze through my hair. I thought of sunrises and sunsets I have seen; places where I have traveled. Within a few minutes, I had several pages filled, each line celebrating something noteworthy. But a funny thing happened once I had listed the obvious, brainstormed all that had ever filled me with joy: I was forced to dig even deeper, to look at the seemingly insignificant with the same delight.

Suddenly, everything became something for which to be grateful. I had a huge epiphany: there is a difference between saying that you are grateful and actually being grateful. We tend to give lip service to the idea of appreciating all that life has to offer without truly living in a state of gratitude. Like the road less traveled, once I began to understand the power of true thankfulness, it made all the difference.

My little book remains open on my kitchen counter, ready to capture my random thoughts throughout the day. Today, the way the sun came through my back doors, illuminating the glittery ornaments on my Christmas tree, made me smile. I want to remember that moment forever, and writing it down somehow elevated that simple experience. Tonight, a fresh salad and grilled chicken tasted like a meal at the Four Seasons. I have come to understand that a well-lived life is not about the big awards for great achievements or the adoration of the crowd. It is about embracing the tiny, mundane experiences which may seem commonplace, but in reality are extraordinary. Woven together, these become the brilliant tapestry of a person's existence.

The older we get, the faster the days seem to pass. It is no great mystery, just simple mathematics, as every twenty-four-hour period, each month and subsequent year represent a smaller and smaller portion of a person's lifespan. That could be a cause for panic, but I prefer to see it as something to celebrate.

Gifts Which Keep on Giving

I have spent the afternoon wrapping gifts. As I tie a bow around each package, I hope that the recipients will be happy to receive them. It is always fun to plunder the attic to see what I have tucked away for family and friends. You see, I am a shopper (and no longer in denial about it). I am on the lookout year-round for the perfect thing for everyone on my list. Sometimes, I fall short, like the boots I bought for my oldest granddaughter one September. They were adorable, just her style, and I knew that she would be thrilled. So imagine the surprise on both of our faces when we discovered that I had bought her two left shoes. (Lesson learned: always check before you leave the store.) But it has become the stuff of family Christmas folklore, a story to be retold every year as we sit around the tree. I dare say the tale is more memorable than the gift might have been.

Presents can be personal, useful, extravagant, homemade, and even the silly ones are wonderful. The fact that somebody cares enough to choose something just for you is a tangible demonstration of their affection. And it is, of course, a nod to the gold, frankincense, and myrrh that the Wise Men bestowed on the baby Jesus so many years ago, a commemoration of the reason for the season. And so, in spite of what the glitz and gaudiness of mall marketing might otherwise indicate, gift giving is a special kind of annual exchange, a thoughtful token of who is important to us.

I have some lovely reminders of holidays past. A friend once gave me a beautifully-bound blank journal. On the first page were the words, "Write beautiful stories with happy endings." I thought of that quiet challenge for months before settling down to write my first (and yet unfinished) tale. And in the years that have followed, I have come to understand that the true gift that year wasn't in the object: it was in the wish for me, the person's belief that I had the potential, the talent, the wherewithal to be a writer. Another friend gave me a lovely bookmark engraved with a quote attributed to George Eliot: "It's never too late to be what you might have been." It came to me one Christmas as I pondered my future, wondering what the next chapter of my personal and professional life might be. I often daydreamed about the possibilities as I used it to mark the pages in whatever book I was reading. And one day I knew with reasonable certainty that I wanted to try my hand at writing. This year, an early present from my bestie was a mug that simply says, "I write. What is your superpower?" I have used it every morning for coffee because it makes me feel good and somehow assures me that I really truly am a budding author. I love it. Of course, there are other examples I could offer, memories of so many Christmases past, but these most recent standouts gave me a new direction, a challenge, a vision.

With gratitude, I set my sails for the course they helped plot for me.

The Perfectly Imperfect Holiday

I have been trying to think of the perfect Christmas idea for two weeks now. In the past, I have written about lessons from Santa and carefully selected presents. I have explored what the holiday means to me both spiritually and emotionally. I have tried to hold tight to the moments, wondering how many more of them I get to share with family and friends. So yeah, I have exhausted all of the possibilities to do justice to this, the most wonderful time of the year. I suppose that it is every writer's nightmare to dip into a dry creative well. It certainly I is mine. And I so want this post to be perfect and inspiring and timely. No pressure, right?

Let's face it: the stress is on from Thanksgiving until Christmas Day. We hustle to make the magic happen, to deck the halls and bake the cookies, to wrap the gifts and attend the parties. We try to cram so much peace and goodwill into one month that often, it is simply overwhelming. Life is not a Norman Rockwell painting. Sometimes, it is quite imperfect.

I have had some absolutely wonderful Christmases, filled with love and laughter. There was the year that my newborn baby came home from the hospital with me in a big red stocking. There are memories of so many Christmas mornings when squeals of delight punctuated the dawn, and later, we shared a delicious meal as we listened to carols softly playing in the background. But I have also had sad ones, when grief and difficulty diminished the moments of comfort and joy. Such is the rhythm of life, I suppose. And yet ironically, it is the fractured celebrations, when tragedy overshadowed everything else that I remember most: the Christmas dinner at Waffle House on the way home to bury my children's father, the car that had to be towed a hundred miles across icy roads when we broke down in the middle of nowhere, the tree that never got decorated after my mother's passing or the holiday that came far too soon following my cancer surgery. Those have become the pivotal chapters in our family's Christmas history, times when we leaned on each other, putting traditions aside, because the holiday spirit was channeled in a different direction. Perhaps that is what made them even more precious.

Life, I have learned, is composed of many experiences, both good and bad, tied neatly with a great big ribbon of memory. And it is quite the gift.

This cloudy afternoon, I plugged in the Christmas tree. It isn't like the big live one we used to have.; in fact, it's thin and leans slightly to the left. The sentimental ornaments, collected since I was a teenager, are still tucked away in the attic. Some of the gifts are haphazardly wrapped. Half of the lights on the garland that surround the patio doors are burned out; the vigil light that illuminates my nativity scene needs a fresh battery; the decorations around the fireplace are drooping; and I still have to get a candle for the kitchen table centerpiece. I look around. It is perfectly imperfect. But I am here, grateful that I can celebrate another Christmas. And I am filled with joy.

Our Savior entered this world from the lowliest of places. And although He was a king, He was born in a stable, not a palace. Certainly the fact that there was no room at the inn was less than ideal. While there are many lessons to be learned from His humble birth, perhaps one of the most important is that sometimes the greatest miracles come from the least likely beginnings. I hold on tightly to that promise.

So maybe this Christmas will be the best one yet. And maybe, this simple blog is the one I was supposed to write all along.

I hope that you will embrace the holidays, whether perfect or not, and may you find happiness, regardless of your circumstances. If someone in this great big world loves you, then, you are truly blessed. Ignore the lumpy gravy, the messy house, the annoying relative. You will laugh at these things tomorrow. Focus on enjoying this precious snapshot of your life, this moment, which is all any of us are guaranteed. That's where the real magic lies. Peace, truly is the greatest present of them all.

Twelve Months of Good Intentions

Once upon a time, I gauged the success of New Year's Eve by how great the party was. I planned the fun, months in advance, as though my future depended on it. Ah, youth. Now, I am more likely to be at home in my pajamas, nursing a glass of wine when the clock strikes midnight than out painting the town red. I guess I must acknowledge the shifting perception that comes with age.

Like so many others, I find myself a little introspective as the new year approaches, reciting the platitudes that we all know so well. Somehow, before the page on the calendar flips from December to January, we drink a cup of good cheer, spoon a heaping serving of optimism upon our holiday plates and liberally sprinkle the dish with resolve as we make a list of resolutions, confident that anything is attainable. We vow to stick to the diet, save some money, and organize our homes. Like that magical night, when Santa manages to deliver a sleighful of toys while all the good little children sleep, nothing seems impossible. And yet, within a few weeks, we often abandon our good intentions and gym memberships as we are forced to confront the reality that change is never easy. That which alters your world as you know it can be uncomfortable and difficult. Trying to achieve measurable goals is often stressful, especially for the self-driven or competitive. So what's the answer? Do we simply give up, dooming ourselves to failure or go along with the ruse, pretending that this will be the year that our intentions are not simply bricks with which to pave the road to hell?

I think there is a compromise. It is much like that proverbial elephant. You simply can't eat him all at one time, right? So perhaps the key to real transformation is in taking baby steps, working on mastering one task before moving onto another. And maybe something as simple as remembering to take out the trash or eating broccoli once a week might be a real triumph. This year, instead of making big promises that I know will be difficult to keep, I am going to make a list of twelve simple objectives, one for each month of the year. Psychologists say that it takes thirty days to make a habit, so with that in mind, if I am able to concentrate on making something new happen during each thirty-day increment, then, I should be able to build upon the success of the previous month. I can only hope that by next December 31st, I will be filled with a sense of accomplishment. Wouldn't that be lovely?

I am going to write each of the following ideas on a slip of paper and put them in a jar. On the first of each month, I will choose one at random and let that be my focus for the days which follow. The element of surprise might make it even more fun and challenging. Here is what I have so far:

1. Learn something new
2. Eat only "real" food, eliminating sugar and junk
3. Exercise daily, even if only for a few minutes
4. Donate clothes which no longer fit me and items I no longer use
5. Meet new people
6. Be mindful of my health and guard it
7. Speak up for myself, by expressing what bothers me and asking for what I need
8. Keep a prayer journal
9. Read at least 5 new books
10. Declutter, especially the "hidden" storage
11. Volunteer
12. Stop trying to multitask by concentrating on one thing at a time
13. Work on Angelique's Legacy
14. Count my blessings
15. Play upbeat music and dance daily
16. Unplug – spend less time in cyberspace or watching mindless tv
17. Sanitize the phone and television remote control on a regular basis
18. Use my imagination in a new way
19. Respect myself as well as others in thought, word, and deed

20. Meditate, in spite of my monkey brain
21. Try yoga
22. Sing daily
23. Remember to appreciate those who love me
24. Finalize "important" papers
25. Fiercely protect my joy
26. Guard my finances by being aware of spending (That means less shopping.)
27. Enjoy the time with family and friends
28. Entertain at home/have a party
29. Don't hold back
30. Redecorate one room
31. Replace the windshield on my car
32. Spend more time outside
33. Manage my energy
34. Nurture my soul
35. Go somewhere that I have never been
36. Place kindness above all other behaviors
37. Forgive someone who has hurt me
38. Accept that which I cannot change and change that which I can
39. Remember to always view the world from a place of love and compassion
40. Keep on smiling, even when I don't feel like it. Better yet, laugh.

Yes, I understand that there is more to this list than I will probably be able to accomplish in twelve months, but maybe I will get industrious and tackle two or three of these at a time. (Sanitizing the tv remote should be a piece of cake.) Some require action, while others necessitate a shift in thinking or a change of heart. Including the abstract as well as the concrete makes sense to me since obviously, the whole point of setting a goal is to develop into a better human being, regardless of the approach. There are folks who have, in fact, given up the whole concept of resolutions completely, opting instead for a word to live by or a mission statement. I like that idea, too. Certainly, such a tactic provides a litmus test by which you are able to measure your attitude and behavior. And repeated often, it can keep you on the road to self-improvement. Growth, even in the smallest of ways, is still progress, right? In my opinion, one of the greatest sources of unhappiness is in being stagnant. None of us are too old or ill-equipped, and it is never too late. Even for me.

    I have often thought that even-numbered years were better than odd ones, that fortune somehow smiles more brightly upon those 365 days which are easily divisible, gifting us with a little more joy, a little more success. The biggest life challenges for me, including my two cancer battles which occurred in 2017 and 2019, have supported that theory. And the banner years of my life have been even ones. Maybe there is something to it. Who knows?

    But like the rest of the world, I, too, am filled with hope on the eve of this new year, a special one which ushers in a brand new decade. Life is always full of promise, dreams to be pursued, days that are yet to be lived, a chapter yet to be written. None of us can predict what lies ahead. And that's what makes it so exciting.

The Twelfth Night

The Christmas decorations are all packed away, except for the nativity scene. I leave it up until January 5th, the twelfth day of Christmas (depending on how you count), the day when the Wise Men visited the Baby Jesus with their gifts of gold, frankincense and myrrh. This is just one of the traditions that has become part of my holiday celebration. And perhaps it is among the most important.

You see, I was "born in the boot." For those of you who have no idea what that means, I am a Louisiana girl. And goodness knows that folks in bayou country honor their customs like nobody else. The twelfth night always heralds the Mardi Gras season, which begins with the sharing of a king cake, a round confection of cinnamon-flavored dough. (It can get fancy, but I am a purist.) At informal gatherings throughout the area, folks share the cake, anxious to discover whose piece has the plastic baby (symbolizing the infant Jesus) which has been baked inside. In some circles, the "winner" is named king or queen for the day. In others, he or she is obliged to throw the next party. Regardless, it is festive and fun.

The holiday is actually practiced worldwide, going back to Medieval times, although not so much in modern America. However, we are all familiar with the idea, having sung the song about the twelve gifts given by a true love on the days following Christmas, even if the last one wasn't a cake. See? It all makes sense, doesn't it?

And on the subject of gifts, I have a few that still have to be delivered to friends that I didn't get to see during the busy holiday. As I removed them from under the tree, I was reminded that instead of being late with my holiday cheer, perhaps I was right on time. Many generations ago, Christmas was a holy day for Cajun families. There was a feast to be shared, certainly, but there was also church and the singing of carols. The old folks thought that the emphasis was to be placed the birth of Our Savior, the celebration of His birthday, and so, the exchanging of gifts took place on New Year's Day instead. It extended the holiday, but it also changed the focus to the true meaning of Christmas. It is an interesting idea. Perhaps in this commercialized world, where marketing is king, we have forgotten Who truly is sovereign.

I don't know about you, but once the holiday hoopla is over, the joyful season coming to an end, I feel a little down. I don't enjoy the steamed broccoli or water with lemon, nearly as much as the cookies and wine. I miss the visits from friends and family whose company seems all the sweeter during this special time of year. I live in Georgia now, and January means "business as usual." It is predictable, boring.

I carefully wrap each piece of my nativity scene, which feels like I am placing a period at the end of the holiday sentence, writing the last chapter in a worthy book. It makes it final, a seasonal door closed until next year. That makes me a little sad, especially now, when each of these occasions is important to me.

This is the time when I miss my homeland most of all. For there, once the Christmas tinsel is tucked away, the party is just beginning. Maybe it is time to start that custom here. The fun is wherever you make it, right?

Words that Start with a C, Part I

I have been thinking about powerful words that begin with the letter C, including chocolate of course. They provide an interesting insight into life.

Take comparison, for example. From the time we are born, the process of measuring ourselves against others begins. In fact, mere minutes after a baby enters the world, it is assigned an Apgar score, a determiner of how ready he or she is to meet the world. As kids, we compare our abilities against those of our buddies on the playgrounds and later, in the sports arenas, giving props, respect and admiration to those with superior athletic prowess. We compare test papers, report cards, SAT scores in school, hoping that we measure up. We look to musical or artistic talent as a way to distinguish ourselves, all the while worrying if we are good, better or best. As we grow into adulthood, we compare everything from the neighborhood in which we live, car that we drive and suitability of the mate we have chosen. Employment status and annual income become barometers for success. And then, there is the undeniable hope that our own children will do well, demonstrate exceptionality, make us proud. I could go on here, recounting lively conversations between women in public bathrooms, as they compare clothing, hairdos and bodies, but I think you get the point. I am sure that anthropologists will assert that there is some deep biological motivation at work here. Perhaps survival of the species is dependent upon comparison as we size each other up, looking for the strongest, brightest and best with whom to mate. Perhaps those whom we add to our pack somehow ensure our safety and contentment. Comparison helps us to choose wisely.

As I work on the manuscript for this book, I think about comparison. I have been careful to choose stories from my blog that are, hopefully, worth reading. But even as I prepare to release it to the world, I am aware of the need for numbers, reviews, stars, all of which are used for comparison to achieve a ranking that will hopefully result in a readership. Like that newborn, who is given a survival score, I always hope that my baby will measure up and thrive.

Part II

So let's continue with this theme of important words that being with a C. shall we?

Competition is a fundamental concept in the Western World. Goodness knows we revere a champion like nothing else. (Superbowl, anyone?) We embrace the idea that anything better, bigger and stronger results from a competitive market. In the workplace and on the sports fields, we push ourselves, often to the point of exhaustion in an effort to triumph, to be more successful, to come out on top in the game of life. And the idea of victory is ingrained in us as toddlers as we are encouraged to run faster, jump higher, reach farther. Yup, everybody loves a winner.

I am reminded of a sculpture I once saw in a fancy high-rise office building. It featured a tall ladder with professional types climbing the rungs. As I studied it, I found it unsettling in its symbolism. One figure was stepping on the hand of the person reaching up from below him. Another was frozen in action, clipping someone in the chin with his briefcase. A woman was hanging precariously, her feet dangling in the air. And two characters stood shoulder to shoulder on one of the treads, pushing each other, a look of frustration etched in bronze on their faces. It was a metaphor, of course, a homage to the dog-eat-dog competitive atmosphere that climbing the corporate ladder fosters. Gee. It sure does make you want to jump right into the fray that rising to the top entails, doesn't it?

So I'd like to offer another C word instead. How about cooperation? What if we saw helping each other as a means of helping ourselves? What if sharing knowledge, resources, and skills meant our own grew as well? What if our neighbor's success enhanced ours? It is a concept that many cultures embrace for survival, right? Why can't we?

Wouldn't it be lovely to sit around with a group of folks, enjoying cup of coffee (or a glass of wine), engaging in a discussion, rather than a debate? Imagine what new ideas we might embrace, what shifts in perception might happen if we didn't always have to be right, if we didn't always need to win? It sure would be nice.

Yet Another Cat Story

I have never had a cat in my life. I hesitate to say "owned" when referencing a pet because let's face it, most of the time, when they come into your life, stealing your heart in the process, THEY own YOU. I can recite the timeline of my existence by the dogs I have loved, starting with Mitzi, a cocker spaniel I had at the tender age of three to Lola, the bijon frises, who is sleeping by my side as I type this. But nope, there are no feline pictures in my family album, no stories of cat antics. Until now.

Several weeks ago, my grandson and I were sitting at the kitchen table engaged in a rather complicated game of Pokemon. The house was unusually quiet as he explained the finer points of how to play, and I basked in the attention that only a seven-year-old can give. Suddenly, he paused and whispered "listen." There was the faint sound of a cat meowing far off in the distance. "Where is it?" he asked. I shrugged, my mind reeling with the possibilities of the kind of mischief a random cat might make. We set out to find the source. He was filled with excitement; I was full of apprehension.

We found the cause of the commotion moments later, locked in the unfinished part of the basement. Somehow, with the holiday hoopla, the comings and goings of busy days and open doors, he had managed to get in and then was unable to get out. At first, I thought him to be the feral cat that had made a brief appearance here a few months ago. We are accustomed to the parade of critters who manage to find their way to our country house, but this one, an orange tabby, was a different color. More importantly, he was remarkably friendly. He rubbed against my leg and purred loudly as though it was the most natural thing in the world.

Obviously, he was starving and quickly found his way up the stairs and into the kitchen, where he managed to scarf down a bowl of Lola's food in a matter of seconds. The collar he wore indicated that he belonged to somebody. Such a sociable cat surely must live nearby, I figured. Once he was done, I shooed him out so that he could return home. But much to my surprise, the next morning, he was sitting outside my kitchen door, patiently waiting for breakfast and a bit of human companionship. I had to admit that his tenacity was impressive.

I called neighbors and posted on social media. Within a few hours, I learned that the cat belonged to a young couple who had recently built a home about a mile away. We loaded him into the truck and set out to return him to his family. They didn't seem at all surprised that he had found his way to our house. Apparently, this is his modus operandi.

"He's an outdoor cat, who loves people and likes to roam," they said. "We call him Concrete. It is what happens when you allow a four-year-old to name the pet."

I chuckled. It seemed an appropriate name for an animal so resilient, solid and strong.

We bid our goodbyes and headed home. But later that evening, Concrete reappeared at our back door, waiting to be invited inside. I was thinking that perhaps I should rename him Boomerang. Was there something special about us, I wondered? It has been almost three weeks since he made his presence known, and I dare say, he thinks he lives here. On sunny days, he can be found napping on the back patio. On cool nights, he snuggles under a pillow on the front porch furniture. He greets us when we leave the house and is often waiting for us when we return. He is a constant presence as he explores the yard. It has been fascinating to watch him hunt for small prey on our property, stalking them like his ancestors might have done. As a result, I suspect that the field mice have moved on to safer pastures. That's a bonus. For a while, we continued to occasionally feed him dog kibble until we ended up with a can or two of cat food in the grocery store cart. Now, he appears to have bonded with us. Maybe dinner is better at our house.

I have been told that while you may choose a dog, a cat chooses you. That may or may not be true, but it seems that Concrete has adopted us as his second family. I must admit I had preconceived notions about cats being finicky and aloof. I thought them to be stingy with their affection. Concrete has proved me wrong. Sure, he isn't really my cat, but honestly, he already has me wrapped around his furry paw.

Let's Agree to Disagree

My momma always told me to avoid discussing politics or religion with folks if I wanted to maintain a peaceful relationship with them. Sooner than later, she warned, a difference of opinion is bound to occur, and it is hard for everyone not to end up with bruised egos and frazzled nerves in the process.

An equally wise man, the philosopher Cicero, put it this way: "the need to compel others to believe and live as we do cripples us, makes us a prisoner of our own negative thought patterns." It's an idea that is as true in our modern world as is was in ancient Rome. Until we can release the desire for others to approve of our choices, we remain stuck. You don't need anybody's consent to be who you are or believe what you choose to believe. But you don't need to turn those opposing views into an ongoing argument either.

Somehow, the desire to be right causes us to become blind and closed-minded, which is never a good way to win friends and influence people. (Thanks, Dale Carnegie.) Rarely is there a positive response to strong-arm tactics or fighting words. And often, the quarrels get personal. Let's face it: somebody always gets hurt during that kind of wrestling match.

In an ideal world, we could disagree well. We would listen attentively to each other's ideas and mutually respect the individual perception from which those beliefs were formed. We would seek to understand first, and then, to be understood ourselves. We would pause to consider all sides to the question before formulating an answer. And we would resolve conflict by demonstrating tolerance and having an open mind. Ah yes, it all sounds so simplistic. But it isn't. Somehow, the distance between expressing an opinion and causing an offense has become shorter and shorter. We live in a sensitivity danger zone, a virtual mine field of hurt feelings disguised as political correctness.

And we want to be right.

Making moral judgements of others because of where they stand on important issues can be destructive and damaging. But it is also terribly unfair.

The profound truth is that it is perfectly okay to not agree. Asking someone else to accept your values may mean that you are requesting that compromise their principles. You are, in essence, asking them to discard what they believe to be fair and true. Is it any wonder that this might be met with resistance?

We don't have to concede on everything to get along, to practice courtesy and consideration. But we do have to demonstrate acceptance to form deeper human connections.

And therein lies the secret.

We are a cooperative society, created to accomplish more together than separately. America was designed to be a republic, dedicated to meet the social, economic, and cultural needs of an ever-changing population. It has never been a utopia; such a place doesn't exist. Everyone won't always be satisfied; in fact, some never will be. That's the honest-to-goodness truth.

However, a house divided against itself cannot stand.

By the way, the quote is routinely credited to Abraham Lincoln, a politician. He wasn't the first to say it., however. It was in fact, spoken by Jesus, a savior. (Luke 11:17; Mark 3:25; Matthew 12:25) And perhaps we have lost sight of that bit of Biblical wisdom. Conflict weakens any country, erodes the morale and destroys all confidence. If we still believe in the national dream, we must become the UNITED States once more. Perhaps it is time to embrace the ideals upon which this country was founded. And we must each do what we can do make it happen. Our future depends on it.

It's Carnival Time

It is Mardi Gras time in Louisiana, and even though I have lived in Georgia for more than three decades, I always miss the mid-winter hoopla, a time to just party and play with wild abandon before lent, the forty days of serious penance and sobriety in preparation for the Easter season. Somehow, I have never adapted to the fact that here in the Peach State, it is just another Tuesday, marked with no fanfare, much less a parade.

I often tried to make it an occasion when I taught high school. I may have brought a king cake to share with my colleagues or played jazz music as my students entered the classroom. Once, I handed out beads and trinkets, and I got a stern reprimand from administration when a few kids caused a bit of a ruckus, tossing them around the cafeteria. How was I to anticipate that?

Two years ago, I was in the chemo chair on Mardi Gras Day, and I brought beads into the infusion room, hoping to make the gloomy atmosphere a little more festive. Most of the patients and staff didn't get it, unfortunately, and except for the nurse who hung the strands on her supply cart, the whole thing fell flat.

Last year, I learned that the cancer had returned just two days before Fat Tuesday, so the day was spent in worried anticipation of what was next, the merry mood replaced with uncertainty and fear. But as I have come to understand, time manages to change a person's outlook on just about anything. Like the waves of the ocean, life ebbs and flows. We have good times; we have bad times. That much i know for sure. And yes, what a difference a year makes.

So this Carnival season, I am making up my own rules for celebrating. I am planning a little party for my girlfriends, an evening of fun and foolishness and food (and wine, of course), because every once in a while, you have to stop acting like a responsible adult person and get a little crazy. Besides, one should never postpone having a good time, right? And if you can share the frivolity with people who truly care about you, that's an added bonus.

I bought fresh flowers and decorated the house in purple, green, and gold. There are clean sheets on the guest room beds, "just in case." I expect that the laughter will last well into the wee hours of the morning, and I am looking forward to it.

I am making gumbo for the occasion. As I make my list of ingredients to buy, I am reminded of the richness of my heritage. The idea behind Cajun cooking is to take something commonplace and turn it into something extraordinary.

I figure that is a pretty good motto for living well, too. Let's face it: most of our days are filled with simple moments, the mundane and the routine. It is up to us to see the special among them, to celebrate each day. It is one of the many lessons that having cancer has taught me. I try to remember it. We all should.

V is for Virus

Two weeks ago, I stopped at a store on the way to the hospital for routine bloodwork, I needed a few things, including a can of Lysol spray. I like the way it makes the house smell ,and the fact that it is a germicide is a bonus.

"If you are looking for face masks, we are out of them," the cashier said, with a bit of urgency in his voice.

I shrugged. "I have enough of those. Don't seem to make my wrinkles go away, anyway."

He looked at me as though I had suddenly grown a third eye. "No, I mean surgical masks," he said. "No hand sanitizer in stock either."

I smiled and laughed it off, trying not to feel foolish. "Of course," I mumbled. "Hope we all stay healthy."

At the hospital, my chemo nurse gave me "the talk" about hand washing and staying away from public places. "You are part of that high risk group," she said. "Be careful."

I nodded and thanked her as she slipped me a few masks "just in case."

Suddenly, the reality of my current situation was made clear:

My name is Paula Millet, and I have a compromised immune system.

At that time, the Coronavirus was something that "other people" had to worry about, folks who had visited China or lived on the West Coast in areas where a few cases had been reported. I shrugged at terms like "pandemic," chalking the whole thing up to media hype. I listened to the conspiracy theories with interest, thinking some to be plausible, while others were downright absurd.

But within a few days, the number of people who had contracted COVID-19 had grown exponentially. A patient with the virus was admitted to the hospital nearest to my house, next door to where I received chemo during my first round of treatment. An employee at the Waffle House near the hospital where I just had the bloodwork done tested positive this week. I couldn't help but wonder if somehow our paths had crossed, perhaps in a store or restaurant. It's certainly possible. Yesterday, officials announced that an elementary school in the neighboring county would be closed for the next two weeks because of exposure. Today, the entire system dismissed students, advising them to stay home until further notice. How many of those children might now be at risk? This isn't just a disease casually discussed on social media anymore; it is real. And there will be consequences.

For the past four months, my friends and I have been anxiously planning our big night out for the Ovarian Cancer Gala scheduled for this weekend in

Atlanta. Like school girls prepping for the prom, we have exchanged texts and pictures of our dresses, complained about not finding cute, yet comfortable shoes, and arranged for the hotel where we had planned to stay up all night. We were positively giddy over the whole thing. But last night, we learned that it has been postponed as a precaution. I get it, but I am still disappointed.

Am I afraid? No. I have arm wrestled the cancer devil twice and taught high school for 36 years. It takes a lot to scare me. But I understand that the threat is real. Sometimes YOU are the "other people" we think things will happen to; so yes, I am in self-protective mode. So far, I still have toilet paper and water, which for some odd reason I have been told to stockpile. I didn't do that, so I hope that the stores are able to replenish their inventory soon. I have online shopping to keep my need for retail therapy in check. I went to Costco last month, so I have enough paper towels and canned tuna to get us through the worst of it. I'm not getting on a cruise ship anytime soon, although I did see one advertised last night for $10 a person per day. It was mighty tempting. I do have a few unopened bottles of hand sanitizer. I am thinking about starting an eBay business. From what I have seen, I could make quite the profit on them. Maybe that will ease the sting from what I have lost in the stock market.

I am no Chicken Little. I am pretty sure that the sky is not falling. This too shall pass. Count on it. In a few months, the media will have other topics for discussion and the talking heads will be sensationalizing something new. But for now, this is real. Err on the side of caution. Stay out of crowded places if at all possible. If you are sick, remain at home. Eat your veggies and get enough sleep. And for goodness sake, wash your hands with soap. Often. For twenty seconds. Use a little common sense. And be well, everybody.

I is for Inspiration

Ah, the Greeks. More than any other culture, we credit them with igniting our love affair with storytelling and its unique ability to immerse us into a land of make believe. It's here that we suspend reality for just a moment as we are transported to a unique time and place. The myths, where gods and goddesses sat on Mount Olympus eating ambrosia and sipping nectar, while they blatantly meddled in the lives of the mere mortals on earth, became the fodder for later tales penned by the greats. And indeed, Pyramus and Thisbe became Romeo and Juliet, which became West Side Story. (Ask Mr. Google: he will give you a mountain of lesser known examples with the same tried and true tragic plot line.) But perhaps the Greek's most well-known aesthetic legacy to us has come in the form of the muse, that ethereal being from which creative stimulation comes. It is an idea that has endured through the centuries. And it is the nine sisters who most fascinate me as I sit down to write and wonder if I can tap into that same bit of motivation as I search for the elusive quality, that abstract notion we call inspiration.

For the ancients, the artistic stimulus came in the form of an incantation, an appeal for the proper muse to show up and wave some bejeweled magic wand to get the imaginative ball rolling. Of course, there was great fanfare and overflowing gratitude when she did appear bearing gifts, and the writer, sculptor, architect or musician was able to make something beautiful as a result. And yes, when she was off being the benefactor to someone else, leaving the poor artist high and dry, it was disappointing. But it also placed the credit (or blame) on an outside source as through the whole idea of inspiration is some inexplicable, supernatural encounter that either happens or doesn't, something that exists beyond our somewhat limited reach. It is a lovely, romantic notion, but it is misguided. My apologies to Homer.

As human beings, we are uniquely created with the ability to think and reason and problem solve. Yes, that's logical, pragmatic even. But we can also feel, and this, my friends, is the source of what inspires us. Our emotional compass may take us on a wild ride on any given day as we register love, anger, jealousy, sorrow, empathy, fear. We mark the moments, both big and small, in our lives by how it ranks on the joy meter, and the happy times are those we remember as we fondly recall them with each passing year. And conversely, we think of the tragic times, when our hearts were ripped from our chests, the physical pain often mirroring the emotional. Yeah, ask people to truly tell you about their lives, and they will describe these moments, bookended, fitting together like the yin and yang of existence.

So inspiration involves being subjected to emotion, feeling in its purest form, allowing yourself to be vulnerable enough to sense it in all of its rawness, and then figuring out a way to translate that to somebody else. It is that indefinable sensation of being one with the fictional tale. a passionate response. In other words, if a writer wants the reader to experience sadness in a story, then he must do so as well. He must dig deep into his own soul to flesh out the sensation of grief and despair, conjuring up the awareness of how that feels. Some will use mood-enhancing music to evoke a sensation or focus on a memory. (Wine sometimes works, too.) For me, I must literally be transported to the time and place about which I write. I have to jump into Sheldon' Cooper's time machine (which originally belonged to Jules Verne, by the way) and "go there" to experience the story, and the accompanying emotion, right along with my characters. As an invested observer, if I am not crying and laughing with them, as they navigate the conflicts or celebrate the triumphs, then I am missing the mark. And it shows. I am fully aware that writing is about a connection between the author and the reader, a moment in time shared between two strangers. I don't take the responsibility lightly.

Inspiration is not a pretty muse perched on my shoulder, whispering the right words in my ear; no, it is the real, down and dirty feeling of what is truly happening as each chapter or experience unfolds. Sometimes, it is really hard, downright agonizing, but it is always authentic. And I hope that translates into what I write.

When I taught high school English, I used to ask my students if they liked to read. Some were enthusiastic while others made a sour teenage face and declared that they hated it. My simple questions to the nay sayers went something like this: "When you read a book, do you see the movie in your mind? Do you feel like you are there?" The nonreaders were surprised that this was even a possibility, that there was more to the process than simply correctly identifying the words on a page. And I am pleased to say, that I was able to convert a few of them by showing them how to let their imagination take over as they explored a work of fiction. (That was a big victory as an educator. Huge.)

And so, it is incumbent upon the writer to set up this world and the characters who inhabit it, to tap into that intangible source of inspiration to show what a book might reveal without telling. If done right, the storyline should allow the reader to use their own perception and experiences to fill in the blanks and ultimately be moved in some way. Sigh. And yes, that is pathos, which means to stir up the emotions. It's a Greek term. Those folks really were literary geniuses, weren't they?

Angelique's World

I have reached "a certain age.". I have a compromised immune system thanks to the cancer devil, and I currently take a powerful chemo pill. Yup, I am in that high risk group. Like so many other folks, I am stuck at home, self-quarantined, and trying to stay healthy in the midst of this pandemic. I am also trying not to go stir crazy.

I have walked the house, looking at all of the projects that I need to tackle, things I have deferred for over a year. I made a to-do list and pinned it to the refrigerator. But my heart isn't in it. I can live another few months with my messy garage and stuffed attic. I contemplated baking cookies and even went so far as to assemble the ingredients. But then, I thought of how hard I have been trying to lose the steroid weight, and I reconsidered. I needed something to keep me busy, something productive and important. For the past week, Angelique has tried to gently nudge me back into her world, calling me to finish her story, the one I began two years ago and then abandoned, left languishing on my computer.

It isn't that I didn't want to write. I didn't think that I could. Chemo brain is real. The massive drugs pumped into your system attack every cell, even the healthy ones, which is why your hair falls out and your taste buds die. I'll spare you the details of the poison's side effects, but let's just say, it compromises your thinking. It certainly did mine. Many days were a complete fog, a one way trip to lala land. No joke.

I didn't feel confident enough to pen a readable novel. And I felt that I owed it to Angelique to wait until I could tell the rest of her story and tell it well. But then, I wondered about time, that commodity which we cannot stop nor create. If I waited too long to write the sequel would I run out of the time I needed to do it? It was a question that haunted me, and I didn't have the answer.

And then, I got an email from a random reader. A few days later, I got another. Then, a recent 5-star review popped up on Amazon. And each one was asking for more of the story. I am a firm believer in signs, and I do think that they come in threes. This was mine. Isn't it funny how a few words of encouragement can often be all the motivation we need? Sometimes, we underestimate the influence we have on each other. Writing is such solitary work that connecting with a reader can be incredibly motivating. Interesting, isn't it?

And so, I began to think once more about the characters that have become such a part of me. The blog has been therapeutic, but it hasn't scratched my itch to write fiction. I can't deny that. I'm not going to lie: It takes me twice as long to write as it did at one time, but that's OK. Progress is progress, right?

I have spent the past two days in my pajamas, lost in Angelique's world. I managed to write 4000 words. The manuscript for *Angelique's Legacy* is now 30,000 words long. I figure that I am a third of the way there. Surely, I can finish this race. Most people don't know this, but I write backwards. I always pen the last few paragraphs of the book before I begin. I need to know where I am going before I can figure out how to get there. This one stirs my emotions like nothing else I have ever written. I can't wait to share it with you all. Wish me luck! I have included the first chapter of *Angelique's Legacy* below. If you have read the trilogy, you will see that it continues from the last bit of *Angelique's Peace*.

Chapter One

Spring, 1875

Aimee exhaled, the sound of it echoing through the silent room. She concentrated on her breathing, a technique she had often employed as she assisted Franklin in surgery during those moments when the gruesome sight of blood and infection was too much to bear. And with each lungful, she willed herself to calm her runaway emotions, as the sound of her heart beat so loudly that she was sure the others heard it as well. It seemed like hours had passed since they had first gathered in the parlor, and she had taken her place on the crimson velvet settee, but it had only been a few minutes, fifteen at the most. Time has a way of playing tricks on the mind at such times.

Her mother, Angelique, had insisted that this, the best room in the house, be reserved for company and important occasions, so when she appeared with the fancy china coffee pot and delicate cups loaded onto a silver tray and invited them to sit, both Aimee and Franklin knew that something significant was about to happen. But something significant had already happened that day and the one which had proceeded it. Uncle Gaston, the man who had once stolen her, ripped her from the busy streets of Charleston as though she was the pocket book belonging to a fancy lady, had resurfaced. And although the passing years had done much to erase the memories, she still had occasional nightmares, moments when she was once again that helpless five-year-old child kidnapped by a stranger. His arrival at the clinic had seemed like an uncanny coincidence, a cruel twist of fate, and as he slept, she gazed at his scarred face, the cracked lips of his mouth twitching with the pain. She mentally practiced the speech, the words that as a grown woman, she wanted him to hear. And she was ready to deliver it. But Franklin, always her protector, had shielded her from him and the loathsome man had passed away far too quickly for her to get the closure she didn't even realize she needed. Aimee wringed her hands. Gaston was gone and never able to hurt her again, but her mother's implication that there was more to the story than neither she nor Franklin knew gave her pause. She couldn't imagine what secrets connected her charming, elegant mother and that wretched creature, but her intuition, honed from years of nursing, told her that it couldn't be good. She closed her eyes and prepared to hear the truth.

The walnut clock on the mantle began its melodious song, marking the half hour. Angelique carefully poured the coffee and cream, then dropped a cube of sugar into the cups. Her hands shook as she handed one to each of them before moving to the chair opposite to where Aimee and Franklin sat. She looked first to Andrew, her husband and father of her children, searching his face, her eyes filled with tears. He had always been her greatest supporter and an ever-present source of comfort. She reached over to take his hand. He nodded and then offered a weak smile. Angelique cleared her throat. There was a long pause, and Aimee thought it odd, that her mother, always so poised and prepared, seemed to be at a loss for words.

"Just tell us what you think we need to know, Mother," Franklin said, "We are not children, certainly."

"Whatever it is, we will understand. You have shown us that the tie that binds our family is strong. We have weathered some difficulties, of course, but as you were always quick to point out, together we can face whatever may befall us. It is one of the first lessons you taught me as a child," Aimee said.

Angelique sighed. "My beautiful, brave children. You do honor me with your loyalty. And however painful it is to tell, you deserve to know the story of the life your mother lived before this one with all of you. As you will soon see, it is quite the tale."

"Before Poppa, you mean?" Aimee asked.

"Long before then, when I was a young girl, living on Chauvin Plantation and the years which followed."

Franklin took a sip of coffee and shifted his weight. She had his full attention.

"I met him one night at a dance held at a neighboring plantation. He was older and brazen in his attempts to get my attention. But there was something mysterious and interesting about him as well, and he swept me off my feet in a matter of weeks. The courtship was brief and the marriage came quickly. As a young bride I adored him, and the baby girl who came into our lives shortly thereafter."

Angelique swallowed hard. She knew that there was more, much more, to tell, and once the box which carefully secured the memories had been unsealed, she would have no choice but to relive them. The moments rolled through her mind like tumbleweed in the desert.

"Life changed when our sweet Josephina went to live with the angels, claimed by the fever. It was as though she was the one who bound us as a couple." Angelique paused, remembering. She wiped away a tear. "Without her, little remained between us. I locked myself away, lost in my grief, and despair. He fell deep into the arms of the devil."

"The devil?" Franklin asked, his eyes growing wide.

"It undoubtedly seemed that way," Angelique said. "I had no idea that he was a gambler, even in those early years together, but as time passed, it became the center of his life. He courted Lady Luck as he would a lover, and she ultimately jilted him. Within a short period of time, the debts became overwhelming, and he grew so desperate that he faked his death, staged an elaborate hunting accident just to escape the financial penalties of his misdeeds. He simply disappeared, swallowed up by a big world, leaving me penniless and alone to sort through the mess he had created. Because of him, I lost Chauvin Plantation and everything else we owned, a tragedy that altered my life."

"And that got you to the resort where you met Poppa." Aimee added. She cleared her throat.

"I am so sorry, Momma. And now I understand why getting your home back was important. How sad for you. How utterly unfair to be burdened by the consequences of another's choices." She hesitated. The story had triggered a recollection she herself had fought to forget. "Uncle Gaston. He gambled, too. Every single day. I didn't understand at the time what playing cards meant. I was so little, and it was hard to sit and wait while he spent hours at the tables. But I remember that some days he would be sad and happy on others. I guess it was tied to his winning."

Franklin furrowed his brow. He remembered the first time he saw Aimee, perched on a high stool as she waited patiently for her uncle to finish his game, finally releasing her. She was so innocent, so fearful. His heart clinched. Those images of little Aimee haunted him, too, but this raised bigger questions in his mind. "Is that why you recognized Uncle Gaston? Did he know the gambler you married, the one who vanished? And did you ever find him? Was he still alive and did you divorce him? I assume you must have in order to have married Poppa."

Angelique took a deep breath. This was the moment of truth. Jean Paul seemed to have been unstoppable, a man resurrected from the dead over and over again. She certainly had believed the men who had carried what she assumed to be his lifeless body home so many years ago. And she thought he was dead for the second time after he rowed away into the raging winds of the hurricane. But the evil one had lived, and once again shattered her life when he stole her precious child, breaking her motherly heart into a million pieces. She had no knowledge of what might have happened to him in the years which followed, but it appeared that he had lived a hard life, reaping the consequences for his reckless decisions. That was justice. But now, he was truly gone, and she had watched him take his last breath earlier that morning. After all that happened, all of the pain and sorrow, it was time that he was finally buried, laid to rest once and for all.

"Gaston is a name he bestowed upon himself, an alias, a change in identity to hide who he really was. In truth, he was Jean Paul LaTour. And he was once my husband."

The silence was deafening, the air in the room suddenly thick and heavy.

Aimee stared into the delicate cup filled with cold coffee. Her mind was reeling, replaying the months spent with the man who had claimed to be her mother's brother, but actually was her husband. "I don't understand," she whispered.

"I know it is confusing, Aimee. And there is more to tell, of course. But for now, let me say that I truly believed him to be dead when I met your poppa. When our paths crossed again on Last Island, I thought we had engaged in a final show down and that he had perished in the storm that had claimed so many. It wasn't until we met Franklin in the park that I learned the truth, his identity confirmed by the tell-tale scar he bore."

Franklin winced at the memory, which had changed his life as well. "I'm not sure who rescued whom that day, but I am glad that I could help."

"You were our hero, Franklin. And most recently, you have proved that still to be true."

"So that means I had an older sister?" Aimee asked.

"Half-sister. But yes, and she was beautiful just like you girls."

"One more question, Momma," Aimee said.

"Of course. Ask anything."

"Were you not going to tell us the truth? Did you not think we deserved to know?"

Tears filled Angelique's eyes as she searched for the words, the justification for concealing something so important. She swallowed hard, unable to speak.

Andrew, who felt that it was not his story to tell, had patiently listened as the drama unfolded, but sensing his wife's discomfort, finally spoke. "Once your momma found you that's all that mattered to her, Aimee. Besides, we figured that he was still in Charleston, or perhaps had gone to France. We had determined that it was best for our family to leave his existence in the past."

Aimee nodded in understanding. She looked to her mother, who seemed to be intent on saying all that was on her mind.

Angelique sat quietly, her hands folded as though in prayer. "There is one more thing." She took a deep breath. "I was prepared to kill him as he lay in your clinic. And I would have done it with little consideration as to the value of his life. Somehow, I thought that doing so would erase the history, his role in my story. But that was foolish. I suppose. I imagined that with him gone, I would never have to face this moment, one I have dreaded for years."

"Telling us, you mean?" Franklin asked.

"Yes, of course. But I learned something important as I sat at his bedside. Unless we can face the demons of our past, we seek revenge rather than truly feeling what has happened to us and all of the subsequent pain it has caused. And that only begets more sorrow. To turn judgment into compassion and vengeance into forgiveness is powerful. And difficult. But that's when true healing begins."

Franklin placed his cup on the tray and moved to his mother's side. He offered a hug. "You are wise and brave." He turned to Aimee. "And now we know the truth. It is finally over."

She nodded. "The truth," she repeated. "And what about Aida? Certainly you will tell her when she arrives next week."

"Indeed. Your sister should know as well. And I hope it won't overshadow her happy mood. We have a wedding to plan," Angelique said.

"Aida will be fine," Franklin said. "She really had no contact with Uncle Gaston, I mean, Jean

Paul, as we did. Besides, we know that she will be so involved in bridal details that it will be no more than a passing story to her. She does love to be the center of attention."

"You know her very well," Angelique said, laughing, happy for a lighter moment.

But before Angelique could even clear the coffee tray, Aimee had excused herself, retreating to the quiet of her bedroom. She paused in the doorway, studying the shadows cast by the afternoon sun. The curtains moved gently in the breeze as she crossed the room and knelt at the foot of her bed. She carefully opened the wooden trunk, casting aside the books and old clothing until she reached the bottom, her fingers searching until she found it, an old doll with matted hair and a faded calico dress. She clutched it to her bosom as she began to cry. "Sarah," she whispered. "Oh, Sarah."

Developing Immunity

❖

Ironically, I have been researching diseases of the late 1800's, not out of some morbid curiosity, but to use as a possible plot twist in *Angelique's Legacy*. At that time, New Orleans was a hot spot for Yellow Fever just as it appears to be at the epicenter of the Corona virus today. And after a bit of reading, I am awfully glad that I didn't live in the antebellum days which weren't nearly as romantic as they appear to be in the movies, especially during a pandemic.

One commonality between the two diseases is that once you have contracted it, if you recover, you are immune to future outbreaks. They once called it being "acclimated," and it put you at a distinct advantage in society. The Yellow Fever returned with a certain amount of predictability in the warm, humid South where mosquitoes carried the virus, spreading it among the general population. And although it was not transmittable by human-to-human contact, the fact remained that it was a terrible threat, taking the lives of a huge portion of society. Having an acclimated status meant that you could care for the sick, run the shops, and man the transportation hubs. You were an employable asset.

Recently, I read an article that suggested that the young and healthy should deliberately expose themselves to Covid-19 in order to develop an immunity, which would allow them to get the economy moving again. I thought the idea to be rather like a scene out of a science fiction novel than some unique idea to save the country, but then, I have read some rather whacky theories about this pandemic. I'm sure you have, too.

Modern transportation has made it possible to have dinner one day in China and the next in New York City. If a potentially life threatening germ happens to hitchhike along on the journey, then, it is easy to spread the disease from one continent to the next. The advantage of living in a modern world has also made us vulnerable.

Certainly, all of us have been touched by this health threat with its physical, emotional and financial repercussions. Perhaps you know someone who has contracted it, or you have been furloughed from your job. Maybe you have simply felt the stress and anxiety of being in quarantine, away from friends and loved ones. As a parent, you probably worry about your child's education. This affects each of us in a different way, but make no mistake there is an effect.

But this isn't a blog about the current pandemic, at least not literally. Instead, I wanted to focus on the idea of immunity. We can all agree that life is filled with ups and downs, peaks and valleys. Everybody loves being on top of that mountain where the view is quite spectacular, but let's face it: the air is thinner up there, and it can be hard to breathe. Often, all we can do is stand still and try not to fall as we pretend to enjoy the triumph.

The real growth, however, happens in the valleys, on that fertile ground where the rivers flow. It is there, where we have to unlearn everything we think we know about ourselves and start all over again. Yes, there is a considerable amount of pain that accompanies uncertainty, especially as it relates to the future, but it is in that place where we gather the strength, wisdom and kindness that we need for the next mountain that we intend to climb. Here, we develop an immunity to the sting of those difficult moments.

Experience is a great teacher. As much as we want to resist, this period of time is coaching us on how to be still and listen. We are learning to be present, to focus on this one moment of solidarity, bringing our full attention to what is going on around us and within us. We are establishing priorities, grasping what is important and true. That revelation brings with it the intrinsic understanding that we will survive this, and whatever else is yet to come. Armed with a sense of protection, the future somehow doesn't look quite as scary.

C.S. Lewis once wrote that we are never sure of our virtues until face our fears and put them to the test. This pandemic has raised both our individual and collective consciousness. We are learning to be courageous, compassionate, and strong, to appreciate all that we previously took for granted. Mastering bravery takes acceptance and faith. It also requires patience and time. Be good to yourself during this challenging, difficult period, building your own special kind of immunity in the process. And remember, there is none as brave and strong as a survivor.

The Peonies

Peonies were my momma's favorite flower. They appeared with regularity (and great fanfare) at all special events and celebrations, whenever she was in charge of the decorations. Because peonies aren't commonly grown in the hot climate of South Louisiana, finding a supply in those pre-internet days was quite a feat. But she was relentless in her search, usually ordering them weeks in advance. Perhaps their scarcity is what made them all the more special. She would take a deep whiff of their heady scent and for a moment escape to some ethereal place of joy. I can remember marveling at how someone could delight in something so simple, but I suppose that was one of the many lessons that she taught me about life.

When she passed away, taken from this world far too soon, my Georgia colleagues sent a lovely floral basket to the funeral home. I was touched by their kindness, but I was also surprised that although wintertime, the bouquet was filled with various colorful spring flowers. As I bent low to smell their fragrance, I gasped. There were four fat peonies in the arrangement. It was a lovely coincidence, of course, which made the thoughtful gesture all the more meaningful.

This week marks the eighteenth anniversary of the move into our current home, one we lovingly built on an untamed piece of property we had accidentally discovered. We had no landscaping, and I readily admit to having a rather brown thumb, so when one of my students gave me a small bush as a housewarming gift, I wondered just how long I could keep it alive. I carefully removed it from the container and planted it in a space where I could watch it grow from the kitchen sink. Much to my surprise, it sprouted leaves throughout that first summer. When it became dormant during the winter, I feared that I had killed it, but a year later, it bloomed, beautiful saucer sized white flowers. Peonies! What a delightful surprise! From that moment on, I anticipated their appearance at springtime.

This has been an exceptionally long winter, especially since most of us have been on quarantine lockdown through much of it, staring out the window on those cold rainy days as we hoped for better times. We have anxiously waited for those warm temperatures to return, having missed the sun on our faces. Given the circumstances, that has made this spring even more special. And it is as though Mother Nature has taken pity on us, putting on quite a show as the earth reawakens from its seasonal slumber. My rose bushes are covered in crimson blossoms. The hostas have sprung from their shallow beds in various colors of green. Some mystery bushes in my backyard are covered in fragrant blooms which perfume the air.

I expect a bumper crop of wild blackberries, based on the sheer number of thorny vines on the hillside. And once again, my peonies are blooming.

They stage their showy entrance just in time for my mother's birthday on May 3, followed closely by Mother's Day. And just as she ordered them up to mark the important moments in her life, I welcome them as we pause to reenter our altered world. Businesses are reopening; churches are once again welcoming their parishioners. We have even spotted a bear in our neighborhood, having woke from its long months of hibernation. The cycle of the seasons illustrates that life goes on, even in the most challenging of times. And through it all, we are still here, resilient, resolved, and optimistic. I have cut a few of the flowers and placed them in vases around the house. I need to be reminded that this moment is something to celebrate. For indeed, it is.

Can We Talk?

The past week has been difficult. I just typed and erased that sentence three times. It seems like such a gross understatement and a poor beginning for this blog, but I can think of no other way to describe the way the tragic murder of George Floyd and the subsequent violent protests have impacted us both individually and collectively, igniting a range of emotions. It has been difficult on so many levels.

And so, I have struggled to find the right words to say at a time when simple rhetoric seems insufficient to capture the heartbreak, the pain of injustice, violence, and cruelty. There are those who would take advantage of the pain of others to move their own agenda forward, causing more chaos in the process. That is disturbing. Watching the news reports has made us all uncomfortable, but so has the silence. We cannot be afraid to talk about issues if we hope to reach the truth or grasp some level of understanding.

Let's face it: we each view the world through our own windowpanes. We form our perceptions of life through experience, culture, background and education so that we can interpret what happens to us and around us. So I wouldn't be so presumptuous as to assume that I know what it is like to live as a minority in America. I can't relate tales of discrimination or malice just because I was born with a darker skin color. I can't imagine how challenging each day might be for people forced to worry about their safety and security or how a mother's heart must ache each time she must send her child out into an inhospitable world. But as a member of the human race, I can try to have compassion because I do understand grief, pain, frustration and fear, all of which are universal. And equally as important, I can listen as you speak, keeping my heart and mind open to what you choose to share with me. This is how empathy begins.

I spent 36 years in a high school classroom with students of various ethnic backgrounds. As the demographics of our district changed, so did the pupil population, and during much of my teaching career, nearly forty percent of my kids were African American. I mostly taught Speech Communication, an elective, that encompassed three grades and various academic levels. I liked to think of my classroom as a microcosm unto itself, and a true reflection of our diverse society. That made it exciting, yet challenging. Early on in my teaching career, I learned the value of ongoing, meaningful dialogue. I encouraged respectful debate and exchange of ideas. When people talk to each other, when they are able to openly discuss what they think and feel, they discover that while there are differences, there are also commonalities. That can be quite the epiphany. Through honest conversation, we can often reach a greater understanding of each other, even on topics upon which we may not readily agree. That takes trust; that takes vulnerability. But that's also when change happens. I have witnessed it over and over again. And it is something to behold.

There is no magical formula for fixing our broken world, no powerful meme that would wake us from the slumber that keeps us in denial and somehow motivates us to sing "We are the World" around a symbolic campfire. In order for change to be collective, it must start with each of us as individuals. But what we do matters; what we say is important. We must each examine our own conscious, look into our own hearts and be honest with ourselves about what we believe, what we honor as a personal doctrine. And then, we must ask the most basic of questions about how we live: "Am I acting out of love?" It seems rather straightforward, a recurring theme among songwriters and authors, a noble idea emblazoned on t-shirts and coffee cups, but it is the most basic of truths. Respect is harvested from a garden planted in love. So is kindness and compassion. We raise each other up when we are able to recognize our mutual humanity. And I think that begins when we form relationships, when we unafraid to get to know folks who don't look like us.

We are told to love our neighbors as ourselves. And there is no mention of color or creed in that directive. In fact, the word "love" is mentioned 551 times in the Bible. Could it really be that simple? I think so.

Perhaps the Beatles were right: "All you need is love." We have already seen where hate has gotten us.

Readers, Reviews, and Rock 'n Roll

If you want to be suddenly transformed into a 5th grader, about to be involved in a playground pick, if you want to question your ability several times a day, have your confidence shaken or boosted at every turn and just plain doubt your sanity on a regular basis, write a book. Why? Partially because of reader reviews, those carefully chosen words, the penned opinions of those who have read your work and, hopefully, deemed it worthy.

I must admit that never paid much attention to the whole phenomena when I was simply a reader of books. And like most folks, I rarely weighed in with my thoughts. But now that I am on the other side of the experience, I understand how important they are, how they have the ability to attract new readers while partnering with a writer as he or she builds a following.

Those recommendations are priceless and the best marketing tool imaginable. But I also have come to recognize how one negative judgment, one poor estimation of the value of those words can scare away the multitudes, leaving a writer dead in the water. We hope those never come.

Because it is so subjective, based on personal taste and perception, there is no way to control the outcome, other than a wing and a prayer (and well written books, of course). The reader is the boss, providing an unbiased evaluation, which makes sense in a consumer-driven area like book peddling.

Honestly, there is nothing more encouraging or uplifting or exciting than to find that someone has left positive feedback. It makes me want to jump up and down, open a bottle of champagne. I feel a sudden urge to run to the computer and type my little fingers to the bone. Yup, a couple of nice phrases cheer me on like a high school band on homecoming night. What can I say? I respond well to praise. Don't we all? I think there is a deeply hardwired human need for approval in all of us.

I often wonder what the greats, Hemmingway, Fitzgerald, Steinbeck (for example) might have done had they written during this age of technology, when a book can be sent to a reading device in an instant and for less than the price of a cup of coffee, anyone can become a literary critic? It is an interesting question, isn't it? Might make for a great short story one day.

As for me, I will continue to write and hope that readers enjoy my stories and blogs. And to all of you who have taken the time to write a review, good or bad, please know that you have made a profound impact on the creative endeavors of that writer. And we appreciate your taking the time to weigh in. We truly do.

And now, please accept my apologies. This had nothing to do with rock-n-roll, but it gave the title a certain ring to it. Maybe it even got your attention. And everybody likes rock-n-roll, right?

BTW... I just bought a new vacuum cleaner. Granted, it is the kind of purchase you hate to make because, well, it isn't nearly as much fun as shopping for shoes. And I did read the reviews, poured over them, in fact, as users touted the benefits of this model and the drawbacks to that one. Public opinion does matter. And yes, my new vacuum cleaner works great

2020 Vision

I recently saw a cartoon of two guys in an H.G. Wells type time machine. One had his hands on the controls, and he said to the other, "Rule #1, never put in this year." And a big 2020 was projected onto a screen. Sometimes, the funniest things are those that hit closest to home, and this certainly does. I think everyone would agree that this year has brought with it unprecedented challenges, leaving us all afraid to ask: "What's next?"

But as someone who is visually deficient, having worn glasses since elementary school, I know that 2020 is perfect sight. A person with 2020 vision is able to clearly see the world, navigate it unaided. So if you bump into obstacles, it is because you cannot anticipate the twists and turns of the road ahead. And in a similar way, perhaps what keeps us stumbling on this slippery slope of a world is the inability to look ahead with optimism. We have been blinded by pessimism.

Human beings are the only animals who are able to consider the future, to look at tomorrow with some confidence that it will be better than today. We can close our eyes and vividly imagine something that is yet to happen. I think that's pretty remarkable. I know that my dog is only worried about the now. She is concerned about her creature comforts and what's for dinner. That's not a bad way to live because let's face it, she isn't consumed with fear and worry. However, it can be a shallow, superficial way of thinking. And if mankind is supposed to be much more evolved as a species, we need to put those powers to work to expand the way we view the remaining months of this extraordinary year by opening both our minds and our hearts.

Thoughts create emotion, so if we view what is to come with anxiety and negativity we begin to experience negative reactions, anticipating the worst. I can recall the dozens of times that I have gotten myself all worked up over situations that were potentially difficult. And often, because I expected them to be awful, they were. I was simply unwilling or unable to consider the possibility that everything was going to be just fine. And I forgot who is ultimately in charge.

On the other hand, if we anticipate something wonderful, we get a nice release of positive feelings. Those experiences that I have looked forward to, a vacation, for example, have filled me with joy, long before the happy day of departure arrives. And when I expected to have a rollicking good time on that trip, most often, I did.

Now, consider that while each of us is processing our future in either a positive or negative light, that energy is released into the world. At the risk of sounding like some unrealistic Pollyanna, let me say that it makes sense to assume that a positive collective mind set is bound to have a domino effect on society in general. As we release millions of imaginary balloons filled with mindful prayers, positive vibes, and good intentions, the heavens are filled with optimism. In other words, if we want the world to change, we have to change it. And it starts with how we think.

Life is filled with mirages, and as we travel the road toward tomorrow, we must trust in the promise that something better waits for us "over there" than what exists "here." What we think is always a choice. And I choose to believe in hope. We can only go forward, right? I have faith that better days are to come. I simply must for my own peace of mind. How about you?

Happy Father's Day

It is Father's Day. Unlike the holiday which honors mothers, this one seems much less commercial. Dad doesn't care about flowers or a sappy Hallmark card. Give him a nice steak on the grill and a six pack, and he's pretty content. If the kids show up, that's a bonus.

The celebration has taken on a different meaning for me as I have grown older. I guess things get complicated by life and twisted family trees. My own father has gone to live with the angels and so has the father of my children. My husband, who did a great job of taking on the role of step dad when my boys were quite young, has no biological children. And now, of course, my grown sons have families of their own, so it is only fitting that they get to decide how they want to spend the weekend. Like I said, it is never easy. But I am confident that somehow we will make it work, and we will manage to be together. At the end of the day, everyone will go home tired and sweaty and satisfied. Who could ask for anything more?

I tend to be introspective at such times. Each annual milestone that I get to witness is a big deal to me, an important occasion. I think being sick has given me a sense of wonder about a whole lot of things and an urgency to share my thoughts in the hopes that one of my "ah ha moments" might also spark something. And yes, I sometime teeter between the ridiculous and the profound. At least I realize it.

Let's face it: when you spend your days trying to visualize your uncertain future, you can get rather reflective. I am not sure if it is chemo brain or the side effects of the meds, but I often get random ideas at 3 a.m., when I am roused from sleep for any number of reasons. The old folks say that time of the morning is the "spiritual hour," when the Divine comes to whisper in your ear and reveal some great truth about life. I don't know if that's a rational theory, but I have had some pretty interesting ideas in the still of the night. And I always feel compelled to share, so here goes:

Quite frankly, the world is a difficult place to live in right now, torn into opposite camps with lines drawn in the sand. People are intolerant of each other, angry over misaligned beliefs. There is so much misunderstanding and hatred. It makes me sad. And I am willing to bet that it bothers you, too. But it isn't like we can stop the earth from spinning and jump off, right? We are stuck here, and we had better figure things out quickly before we do some irreparable damage.

So on this Father's Day, I ask that you take a moment to talk to the Big Daddy of us all, the God of Creation, who must be so sad over what has happened to this world that He loves so much. Like any other Papa, He wants the best for His family, but He also wants for His children to get along. Ask for His guidance. Start with the prayer that begins with the words "Our Father." I am thinking that might be the best present we could possibly give Him on this day when we honor the man who gave us life. Keep the faith, everybody. Right now, it is our best chance of saving this country and each other. And certainly, although imperfect, it IS worth saving.

And Happy Father's Day to those men who are shaping the lives of children everywhere. It is important work that you do. Remember that!

Cancerversary Number Three

Life can change in an instant, the quick blink of an eye. I think that's one of those universal truths that we all nod in agreement with when we hear it said.

On July 3, 2017, my world was forever changed. Three words, "You have cancer" followed by the compound adjective, "late-stage," sent my head spinning, my heart beating wildly. I tried not to cry as I sat stone still, nodding like one of those silly novelty dolls you place on the dashboard of your car. The doctor, who delivered the diagnosis, seemed rather clinical and matter-of fact and I remember thinking how unfortunate that all of those years of medical school hadn't taught him how to soften the blow for his patients. Of course, I also now realize that the biggest moments in life are subject to your own memories, but it is hard to forget even the most minute details of that day.

Quite frankly, the news was unexpected, in spite of some vague and troubling symptoms. I had been blissfully ignorant of what was happening inside of my body; I had taken my good health for granted. Yes, in those days, illness, like death, occupied its own little compartment, far away from the forefront of my mind. It was the kind of thing that happened to "other people." Not me.

Let's face it: we have all had tough experiences, times when we can't think or breathe, where the world stops spinning for a brief period and all we want to do is turn back the clock so that we can "fix" what has happened, return to the time before heartache came knocking on the door. If we could slip into a time machine, we would avoid that car accident or change that foolish decision or save a loved one. We would make everything right again. But, of course, that's not possible.

Sometimes, we are lucky. We get to fix things, start over, but sometimes we don't. And at the risk of sounding like a cliché, that's when you have to adjust your sails.

I am going to be perfectly honest here: having cancer is like being chased by a shadow. Even on cloudy days, it never goes away. In the still of the night, the ghosts and goblins come to visit, their raspy voices taunting you with questions about what lies ahead. You worry. And in truth, it can be a rather frightful mystery, because even the medical folks don't have all of the answers. When cancer takes up residence in your body, it sits on your chest like a huge elephant, making every breath a chore. But that also makes each one a miracle.

I have learned that acceptance isn't resignation. When you are able to recognize that a set of circumstances simply "are," you have to give yourself the grace to actually feel the pain of the emotion and sit for a while with your sadness. But once that is done, you discover a strength you didn't know you had. Seriously. Working through the difficulty of a challenging time is a process, one that is uniquely part of the human experience. But it is here that you discover who you are, that all the assumptions about your frailty are proven to be false. That's pretty remarkable, if you ask me.

When uncertainty is replaced with hope, it brings with it a new reality. You begin to tentatively look at your tomorrows and allow yourself to think that you might just get to celebrate another birthday, plan another vacation, enjoy another holiday. You prioritize. Life looks different as you learn to make space for other experiences, and yes, it is also more precious.

I once heard that prayer is often followed by the conjunction "and." It's true. We pray and fast; we pray and take our medicine; we pray and wait for answers. I pray and remain optimistic. After all, on that fateful day in July, I was told my prognosis was grim, that my moments on this earth were numbered. Fortunately, God had other plans.

Cancer has been quite the plot twist in my life. That much I know. And while I thought that I had spent the past three years trying not to die, I think the reality is that I have spent them learning how to live. And that's the blessing in the storm.

Unplugged

It is Saturday morning, and I, like so many of you, have just reviewed my ever-present to-do list, trying to choose the least distasteful item to tackle first. Laundry? Bathrooms? Grocery shopping? Instead, I pour myself another cup of coffee and check Facebook, then email, browse ebay and Pinterest. Finally, I turn on the TV. The hosts of Good Morning America proudly proclaim that it is "national no-text weekend," and then launch into a lively discussion about how difficult turning our backs on even one phase of technology can be. I agree. We live in a techno-world, a virtual black hole of a time vacuum, where hours can evaporate right before our very eyes. And we stay constantly connected wirelessly via cyberspace and text.

Now don't get me wrong, technology has revolutionized the world, which in itself is a good thing. I am researching the Civil War for my current novel, and asking Mr. Google about specific dates and places has been a godsend. But like any revolution, there will be casualties, spoils of war. And for so many of us, our interpersonal and intrapersonal relationships have suffered.

We substitute emojis and text-speak for real phone conversations. (My grown children already know that if I call, it is an emergency, since I learned long ago that they rarely pick up when their cells ring.) We have fewer face-to-face encounters. And as a result, the art of casual conversation has been lost, altered forever as meaningful dialogue, heart to heart talks, have been replaced by quick posts and hastily scribbled messages, followed by the "send" button. Enter a busy restaurant on a Saturday night, and you will find a phone at each place setting, as essential to the tableau as a fork and knife. God forbid we should become disconnected. And in the process, we ignore the real-life, living and breathing dinner companions, who sit across the table. Even in places like supermarket check-out lines, airport and hospital waiting rooms, where strangers used to connect in a brief moment, you will find people desperately clutching their devices, oblivious to the world around them. This, my friends, is the true zombie apocalypse that some of us fear.

But perhaps the biggest victim in all of this busyness is ourselves as we sacrifice self-awareness, altering our perception in big ways. We don't know how to be still, how to quieten our own minds long enough to be lost in thought, to explore who we are, to free our imaginations. We feel the need to fill every waking moment and as a result, disconnect from ourselves (while ironically, plugging in and connecting to the world wide web.) And as a result, we are influenced by the technological images which are always pushing the next big thing, somehow convincing us that we are always a step or two behind, not quite current or relevant (or good enough). We forget how to be present, to appreciate the sound of a bird chirping or savor a cold glass of tea on a hot summer day. The precious moments escape us, and we are the losers because of it.

So I have revisited that to-do list. And I have added to it. I will take a quiet walk in the woods, without Pandora blasting in my ears or my phone, just in case somebody needs to be in touch. I will light some candles, take a long bubble bath, and enjoy the quiet time. I will experiment with a new recipe, inviting those whom I care for to join me for food and a bit of idle chatter. I may even try to meditate if I can calm my monkey brain. And please don't text me. I won't answer until Monday morning.

Deadly Disasters

There have been many historical events which have changed us as a society, altered our perception of the world in which we live. Many of these are the result of man's temporary insanity... wars, mass murders, hate crimes, genocides (not including zombie attacks here, although they seem to be all the rage these days. These are the product of evil-doers, whose uncontrolled rage result in tragic loss of life and alter our sense of security. But sometimes, they occur naturally. Volcanos, earthquakes, tornadoes, and hurricanes come to mind. And they too shake us to the core, rendering us helpless as Mother Nature releases her fury, leaving death and destruction in her wake.

Today marks the 160th anniversary of the Last Island Hurricane, one of the first recorded natural disasters because of the massive loss of life and property. It changed the topography of the island, leaving it bisected, smaller, vulnerable. Today, it barely exists. But if there is good to come from these moments, it is that it has raised awareness and created a need for early warnings. The scientific community often responds to such a need to guard the public welfare, studying cause and effect, to help us understand our world more clearly. Today, meteorologists and geologists work tirelessly to monitor disturbances in the earth's patterns, serving as sentinels, helping to keep us informed and safe.

But as a writer, I am ever-mindful that there is always the human element, the story behind what happens as a result of these times: the family, who has lost everything; the lovers, who are separated by death; the heroes, who risk their own lives to save others. These fascinate me (and others, I think). The ruins at Pompeii, for example, draw visitors from all over the world, who stand in wide-eyed wonder at the remnants, the fragments left behind. We imagine the people who endured that terrible time and marvel at the horror. Like a train wreck, we want to look away, but can't, fascinated by the picture it paints.

And it was this same idea that motivated me to write **Angelique's Storm**, a fictionalized account of the Last Island hurricane. Three subsequent books came from this original title, and I got to explore the consequences of a man-made disaster on the characters. I always become engrossed in the research as I enter this make believe world which meshes the real with the fiction.

Scan Day

Every six months, I drink a vile potion of barium mixed with some sort of artificial flavoring. The berry is the easiest to force down, although I have recently discovered cappuccino, which is a close second. I extend my arm and a nurse searches for a good vein into which to inject the radioactive dye. After several pokes, I suggest that they use my port. They aren't trained to access it in this department or so I am told. Ah, modern medicine with narrow specialties. The lights are dimmed, and I sit quietly for an hour while the stuff makes its way through my circulatory system. It can't be good for me to have that kind of poison in my body, I figure, but I am left with little choice. Finally, I am led into the procedure room where I am told to lie on a narrow table which slowly moves through the long tube, taking pictures of every inch of my body. The process seems to take forever, and I make use of the time humming show tunes. I am grateful that I am not claustrophobic. Of course, I talk to God, praying that the film doesn't light up like the Christmas tree at Rockefeller Center.

The technician helps me off the table and tells me to drink lots of water over the next twenty-hour hours. Then, he launches into his spiel about the results being forwarded to my oncologist. I mentally calculate when

I might be notified, factoring in the number of folks whose hands must touch the report before it is marked official. The waiting is the hardest part. If I had patience, I'd be a doctor. Yes, I know, bad pun. I may have used it before. Sorry.

Most people happily exist without knowing what could happen, what uncertainty awaits them. They don't think of adverse outcomes or fret about sinister possibilities. They don't worry about tomorrow and freely live in a place called denial. No, they don't fear that which has not yet happened. Gee, I envy those folks. I used to be one of them.

When you have cancer, you are robbed of peace, forced to live on the edge. You have walked over a threshold you didn't know existed into a new place where life is different. Completely different. Your neatly ordered days have been rearranged, and you learn that in the blink of an eye, everything can change because, well, it already has. Certainly, our bodies are hardwired to want to survive, so we listen to the internal rhythm, focus on each labored breath, each random ache or strange symptom. We embrace life as we stay spiritually connected. (Warning: analogy ahead.) Experience always alters perception, but let me put it this way: it is kind of like being abducted by pirates. Forced to walk the plank, you stand on the end of the board surveying the churning waters of the Cancer Sea below. You try to determine if you will be able to untie the restrains, Houdini-style, and then, wonder how far you can swim. Oh, and did I mention the sharks? Of course, you pray for a reprieve, a last minute dispensation that escorts you back into the boat and hands you a mug of rum. Yup, that's a pretty accurate description of scan day.

I have lost count of how many of these exams I have endured. I know that I have had seven of the big ones, with the fancy equipment and the huge copays. And there have been the less complicated ones, progress reports, so to speak. To break the ice with the technicians, I always make my standard joke about wondering when I will begin to glow in the dark. Most try not to roll their eyes. I am sure they hear it on a daily basis. Here is my scorecard: twice, I have received the phone call with bad news, and the other times, I have celebrated a good report. Like Forrest Gump's box of chocolates, you never know what you are going to get.

I live in a lovely bubble of gratitude. No joke: it is quite the magical place to be. I know that given my diagnosis, each moment is precious, and I try not to take anything for granted. A clear scan gives me permission to exhale, to embrace my days with gusto. Well, at least for the next six months.

Keep me in your prayers, will you?

I haven't written in a few months. Each time I tried, I lost my motivation, the wind knocked out of my sails faster than I could type a title. I blamed it on chemo brain, which is no joke. My thoughts are often a jumbled mess, which doesn't translate to writing something profound or even understandable. And since I am mostly chronicling this cancer journey, quite frankly, the subject matter got tedious and repetitious. I figured if I was getting depressed reading it, so was everybody else. Sometimes, I have to press the pause button, give myself some grace. But I have an occasion to mark, and this is the best way I know to do it.

Third Time's the Charm

It is hard to quantify a feeling. We are asked to rank physical pain on a scale of 1-10, and yet, when the heart is breaking, when the emotions run deep, there is no objective way to describe it because somehow, words seem insufficient. We give a label to things because we must call them something in order to give them meaning. There is the idea that naming something gives it power, including the power to hurt us. And so, you sit with that emotion, trying to calm the fear inside, the thing that makes you want to run, even though you know there is no place to hide.

If that sounds dramatic, it is because for me this is a dramatic moment, a place revisited too many times. I am reminded of that 90's film *Groundhog's Day*. Gee, I hated that movie. So yeah, by now, you have probably guessed that I got bad news following my scan. The alien is back, and this will be my third battle with the monster that has chosen to take up residency in my body. Maybe the third time will be the charm. What the heck does that mean, anyway?

It's funny, isn't it, that I avoid using the word "cancer" when I refer to my illness? I sidestep it in this crazy dance I do. I hate the word, its connotation dark and threatening. It is the Big Daddy diagnosis, the one that sends you into a tailspin, with nothing but negative implications. Let's face it: we have all been sick. Perhaps you have had the flu, an appendectomy, a kidney stone. It is intense, awful, but eventually it's over. (Hopefully.) Cancer isn't neat and tidy like that. It is brutal, relentless in its desire to destroy your body.

And it sucks.

We have all been taught that if we can dream it and believe it, we can achieve it. We are assured that a bit of positive thinking can cure disease while creating a place for us to be whole. But that's a bunch of bull. We do have limits, and that, of course, is part of being human. Sometimes, they simply show up at your door, uninvited. Sometimes, they result from your own choices. But as I have learned in the past three years, those limits force us to dig deep, to find solutions, to discover who we truly are. Somehow, we have to work with what is instead of what we wish it to be. We have to embrace reality, whether it is easy or difficult. And we have to learn to love this life, even the imperfect parts.

So here I go again, strapping on my armor, preparing to fight once more. I know the battle plan by heart by now. And I have become quite the warrior. My General continues to protect me as I march through the Valley of the Shadow. And I fear no evil; not even cancer.

Send me all of your positive thoughts and keep me in your prayers. I draw strength from them.

Let There Be Light

I wanted this to be about something other than cancer and medical appointments. Sometimes, I need to stop this merry-go-round I seem to be on and focus on other things. I am to have a biopsy in a few days. It is a tedious procedure, and I don't look forward to it, but I am also impatient, ready to get on with what is necessary to get this treatment show on the road. My life depends on it. This has been an unpreceded year, a confusing time for all of us. For me, the collective challenges seem to compound the personal challenges I am currently facing. But I guess we all have seasons of joy and seasons of pain. We must have faith that tomorrow will be better, but we have to make it happen.

Darkness is the absence of light. Before you stop reading because I have just stated the obvious, let me elaborate. I think it is quite the metaphor.

The only way to get rid of the darkness, that void which makes us stumble and lose our way, it to fill the space with light. Then, suddenly, the path we travel is illuminated. In that same way, if we are able to replace that which is evil and painful with that which is good, we can somehow move out of gloom and into a place of hope.

Yes, I know, that seems rather simplistic, but most real truths about life are, right? We tend to complicate things while we throw up our arms, raging against the unfairness of it all. And we accomplish nothing.

I have learned that whatever we search for, we find. We set up expectations for what is to happen based on our own sensibilities. If we look for ways to be offended, there will be plenty to upset us, and we can scribble lots of sticky notes with negative labels written on them to attach to situations and people. The world becomes a cold and hostile place if that is what we presume it to be. And many folks do.

Conversely, if we believe that there is joy and beauty to be found here, if we imagine that others do care, we can discover a little oasis of connection. That's the key. And it begins with telling our stories, I think. We encourage bravery in each other when we lean in and offer nonjudgmental listening. Let's face it: it is hard to hate somebody whose background you know, whose experience you have come to understand and acknowledge. We need to talk about what has happened to us because, quite frankly, it makes us feel less alone. Through sharing, we learn that we are all human with common moments of pain and triumph. It is a way to start to build a relationship, as we gaze into each other's eyes and whisper, "I see you." And as a result, we are able to embrace the idea that it is possible for all of us to live in unity.

Sure, we can make better policies, launch campaigns. We can take to social media and listen to the talking heads, but what will ultimately make a difference in how society operates is the association. Person to person, group to group. Once we stop making blanket assumptions about each other and begin to talk, we will see change. Love really is in the details.

We all have a little bit of greatness and goodness inside of us. The two qualities coexist. And it is important that we discover those merits in ourselves, acknowledge that we were made to grow a little bit each day. But it is also up to us to discover that in other people. Then, we create a fertile ground for mutual respect.

The world is a big place with things that make us afraid and sad. But that's nothing new: it always has been a relatively scary place. But if we can stand together, even in times of uncertainty, we can begin to understand each other. There is comfort there. Evil exists, and it seems to be magnified during days of strife, but good is much more powerful. Yes, there is darkness, but if we look for it, we can also find the light. It is the only way that we are going to survive these challenging times. But more importantly, that's when we begin to understand the sacred shared experience of this human journey.

I'm Not Old: I'm an Antique Little Girl

I'm still on a little break from writing about cancer. Actually, I cheated here. This is something I wrote fourteen years ago and recently discovered on an old flashdrive. I had to laugh at how I viewed the world and myself at the time as I lamented about being seen as old. I was in the prime of my life then, but perception is everything, right? I've learned so much since then. Now, I am grateful for each birthday.

It began with an allergic reaction to a wasp sting. I sat in the dermatologist's office clutching my puffy wrist, marveling at the shape and size of my fingers. I was there for a simple cortisone shot, which would restore my hand to that of a normal human being. The doctor entered, muttered his perfunctory greetings, and asked the usual questions. He ordered the injection and scribbled a few notes. Feeling uncomfortable by the silence, I made a joke about the pictures of unhappy wrinkled faces which dotted the walls of the examination room. Each warned of the dangers of sun exposure and smoking.

"That's quite a dose of reality there," I commented.

"Yep," he responded. "Are you interested in getting rid of yours?"

"My what?" I asked.

"Your wrinkles. We have a great doctor in the practice who can fix you right up with a chemical peel or laser treatment. A little Botox for those frown lines and some Restalyne for those nose to mouth lines and you'd look ten years younger."

I tried to paste on my bravest smile. *My wrinkles?* I thought. *Gee. Were they that obvious? Had I scared the poor fella with my lined face?* "Let me think about it," I replied, as I pulled down my pants to present my bare butt for the cortisone shot. It was an act of defiance: little did he know that I considered it a symbolic gesture.

I sat in the parking lot examining my face in the rearview mirror. There was no denying that I had some crinkly parts. After all, I was older, had raised three boys to manhood and had spent 35 years in a high school classroom. My life had been a roller coaster of stress. I got summers off for good behavior and had spent more time in the sun than I would readily admit, but was it so obvious that a doctor would suggest unsolicited treatment? Had I committed the ultimate sin: had I managed to grow old ungracefully?

A few weeks later, I went to the dentist for my routine six month checkup. I love my dentist, who has faithfully tended to my oral health for over 20 years. But as old gives rise to the new, he had taken in a new partner, a young hot shot, fresh out of dental school, with a quick wit and a ready smile. In order for this new Dr. Wonder to meet all of the established patients, he was to perform my exam. He opened my mouth and closed it three times; he raised my tongue, first to the left, then, to the right; he made me smile with clinched jaw. I felt like the Cheshire cat. As he examined my teeth from every angle, I was impressed. *He is so thorough; I'll bet nothing gets past him,* I thought. First, he addressed the hygienist. "This is a classic case, and she is the perfect candidate. This is what you are looking for."

My heart began to race – a classic case of what? I imagined myself smiling a toothless grin: was I about to lose all of my teeth? Finally, he spoke to me: "Hmmmmmmmmmm. Have you ever thought about straightening your teeth? Invisiligns would make it possible for you to get rid of that overbite in about seven months. And those crooked bottom teeth would straighten out nicely, too. I'll even throw in a free whitening when you are done."

Rarely speechless, I managed a weak smile. "I am a bit old for braces," I stammered.

"Don't be silly," he replied. "We fit lots of older women. When your teeth are aligned, it will make your face look better."

I jumped up from the reclining chair and almost tripped on my own feet. "Oops," I mumbled when I realized that I was supposed to be whisked back into the upright position. "I'll think about it," I replied, as I grabbed my purse and hurried out the door.

Once more, I did my parking lot exam. I grinned at myself in the rearview mirror. I had inherited my toothy gap from my grandma, which I had managed to close with $25 worth of ortho bands I had proudly purchased off the internet. I was smug about my frugal alternative to costly orthodontic work and as long as I slept with those bands tightly wound around my two front teeth, I was a gapless wonder. And yes, I had my daddy's slight overbite, but at least I hadn't gotten his tendency to freckle all over, so I figured I had hit the genetic lottery when I considered the alternative. I had been to COSTCO where I bought the supersize package of whitening strips and used them regularly. They had transformed my teeth from dull to semi-brilliant, or so I thought. And hey, at least they were my own teeth. Had I been innocently flashing a hideous smile to strangers and loved ones? Suddenly, I was in a bad mood.

So like a good middle aged woman should, I took myself to the gynecologist for my annual visit. Legs in the stirrups, my 30 something doctor began to question me about my health.

"Libido?"

"What's that?" I replied.

"Hot flashes?"

"Every 45 minutes."

"Weight gain?"

"Isn't that obvious?"

"Bloating?"

"uh-huh."

"Mood swings?"

"Just ask my husband."

"Depression"

"Getting there with every question."

After telling me to sit up, she reached for her prescription pad. "You are too old for hormone replacement therapy, so I am giving you a prescription for something that might help you."

"What is it," I asked?

"It is a low-dose anti-depressant. I want you to take it, and then follow up with me in six weeks so that we can monitor your progress."

I managed a half smile as I reached for the piece of paper with the dosage hastily scribbled in Latin.

"I need to think about this," I quickly responded as I stuffed the prescription into my purse. "and don't forget your bone density test," she said over her shoulder as she hurried off to meet her next patient.

So I sat in my car with the motor idling, having one of my serious self-talk sessions. Me? On antidepressants? I prided myself on having survived some difficult life moments without chemical intervention. Nasty divorce, parents' deaths, job stress, money woes, rebellious teens…. None of those things had made me resort to "mother's little helpers." Maybe I really did need them. Maybe I would be a kinder, happier person if my dopamine levels were altered a bit. But maybe, just maybe, I was fine just as I was. Surely I would survive "reverse puberty" with my dignity in tact just as so many women had for centuries before me. I tore the prescription into hundreds of little pieces and threw it into the passenger's seat like confetti. Great, now I would have to add vacuuming the car to my ever-present to do list.

Yup. I have arrived. I have discovered the dirty little secret that no one wants to talk about. I have stumbled upon the lesson that every woman learns, but rarely shares. I have been initiated into the sisterhood of the droopy pants, the pre-Depends generation. I have entered the unnatural state of female aging. I am an older woman in youth-obsessed America and somehow, that's not O.K.

These messages come to us in subtle ways, like a doctor, who suggests an improvement or a teenage hostess who calls us "hon" as she escorts us to the least visible section of the restaurant. Advertisements tout beauty products guaranteed to make us look ten years younger. Older women are told to reinvent themselves, suggesting that the original model no longer works. We are encouraged to make big changes in the way we eat, dress, exercise and work because we must constantly be evolving into something better, something younger. After all, it is the American way.

But sometimes, the message is more blatant. During my last year as a teacher, a younger male colleague routinely commented on how I had "taught Moses." He often greeted me in the mornings with, "if it isn't the old lady. How old ARE you?" Ironically, if he had called me a "workplace whore," I could have slapped him with a sexual harassment suit, but jokes about my age are wrapped in "just kidding" paper and are expected to be cheerfully accepted.

The fresh-out-of-college bunch speak to their older female co workers in the most patronizing way. They snicker as we muddle our way through the latest in techno-training and mock our serious work ethic as they are the first out the door at the end of the day. They claim to work smarter, not harder, a slogan which came to them via Twitter or Pinterest. And eventually, the younger set wins out as employers soon learn that they can hire two twenty-somethings with no experience for one fifty-something with a proven track record.

Only in America is getting older a cause for distain rather than celebration. If I lived in France, I'd be hailed for my maturity and encouraged to take a young lover. If I lived in Italy, I'd zip around on a Vespa in my Prada shoes, never once considering my image to be ridiculous. If I lived in Japan, I would be the revered wise one, whose devotion from her sons and daughters-in-law would be limitless. But I live in American, and I am invisible.

There is a medical anomaly in which certain patients suddenly wake during surgery. Paralyzed by a component of the anesthesia and unable to communicate their pain and fear, they must simply endure until the whole ordeal is over. Sadly, growing older as an American woman is a lot like that. And unless we being the dialogue, nothing will change. We must demonstrate that there is as much power in wit and wisdom as there is in youth and beauty. We must celebrate the lines on our faces, which tell the story of a well- lived life. We must stand up for ourselves and our daughters. We must prove that there is truth to Robert Browning's statement, "Come grow old with me; the best is yet to be."

Take My Hand

A study conducted a few years ago had subjects receive a mild shock when certain images appeared on the screen. After a few moments, the participants, in anticipation of what was to come, began to experience rapid heartbeat, the classic sign of fear. Then, they were allowed to hold hands with a loved one. Their breathing calmed; the stress response was markedly diminished. None of us should be surprised by this. We have all been in scary situations where the comforting presence of someone who truly cares for us made a difference.

And this seems to be a universal phenomenon, a human response to stress. In fact, in various cultures around the world, the folks who live the longest are those who have a support system, people who rally around in cooperation. There is a community response to individual tragedy, the casserole brigade that shows up with food and love and a sympathetic ear. It takes a village, not just to raise a child, but to bear a personal burden.

Like many westernized countries, we have moved away from that collective mentality. Families no longer live in a home together and are sometimes spread out, relocating to distant places because of work commitments or in search of a more exciting lifestyle. Here in America, we are taught to "mind our own business." When placed in situations which require compassion, we find it difficult to know what to say, and so we often remain silent, run away, fearful that if we try to reach out we will be misunderstood. And then, there are the folks who worry that trouble is contagious, so they avoid you like the plague. It is a true predicament.

But it also can be difficult to form real, meaningful human bonds, you know, the kind that last. Some of us are blessed to have "first responder friends." These are the folks who are there when things get messy, who cross the crime scene tape to stand by your side. They stick around, regardless, and you treasure them for they are worth their weight in gold. But those non-romantic soulmates are also rare. Few people love you without a laundry list of conditions. I once read that if you have three true friends, three people whom you can call when you need them, you are indeed fortunate. It raises an interesting question, doesn't it?

We are told that a burden shared is a burden halved. Makes sense. A good support network is crucial in times of personal crisis, and yet, it can be a challenge to draft an army who is willing to take up their weapons with you and "have your back." I know that I have certainly learned a lot about my relationships since I have gotten sick. Friendships evaporated into thin air within months of my initial diagnosis, leaving me to mourn our history, as I wondered what I had done wrong. Even some family members have been emotionally distant and unavailable. So yes, those lessons have been difficult, heartbreaking at times. Quite frankly, few people are willing to stay the course and hold your hand when the ever-present threat of a mild shock is there. Perhaps they, too, are afraid. I get it. But there have been others who have stepped in to wipe away my tears and listen to my litany of woes. I am ever so grateful for their loyalty.

There is one fact which remains, however. Most of us understand that f I can make you feel better, I'll feel better, too. We are biologically wired for empathy, even if it is uncomfortable. And most of us find ourselves compelled to help when we see someone in pain. There is much to be gained from supporting those in need. Perhaps if we remember that, we can begin to make this world a better place.

"Do not fear" appears in the Bible 365 times. Ironic, right? Perhaps we should be reminded daily to be of good courage. Sometimes, the worse things get, the more challenging the experience, the harder it is to feel loved. But if you are really lucky, there are people there for you during those painful times.

The Good Patient

I am a good patient. I make polite small talk with the medical folks and bake cookies for the nurses. I smile and say "thank you" after they have stuck me with a needle. I try not to call too often to ask about test results, and go to my appointments, on time, I might add, prepared to take notes so that I can be labeled "compliant." I even dress nice for chemo and scans. Somehow, in my mind, if I am pleasant enough, show appreciation, and act agreeable, they will consider me worth saving. Yeah, I know, it is a whacky way of thinking, but I can't shake it. Let's face it: as children, we are given messages that how we perform is who we are. Approval is tied to good grades and decent manners. Having athletic or musical prowess is a bonus. I am not sure that we ever discard those messages.

We have been taught that if we follow the rules, be respectful, polite, and kind, life will treat us well. But the effect/cause dynamics of that idea flies out the window when things go awry. And let's face it: at some point, we will all have to turn and face the ugly demon of tragedy, who appears at the doorstep and manages to gain entry, even if we have been diligent to guard against it. You can't outsmart pain or outrun it. It comes and often, it keeps on coming.

And sometimes, it keeps you from being authentic.

While you are performing your tap dance of positive vibes and grateful attitude, those feelings of pain and grief are pushed deep inside. But they don't go away: they just sink to the bottom like a rock that has been thrown into a swimming pool. And every so often, you have to dive in and clear them out.

That's what I have been doing. This is what I am currently facing: the cancer is back in the same spot as it was a year ago, and this time it is hell-bent on causing trouble. It is an offspring of the one that was removed, something they call a "sanctuary tumor." I always thought that was a nice adjective, but not in this case. It seems that the thing has found a hospitable place, one that my body isn't trying to evict it from, creating instead a comfy environment for it to reside. It quite possibly is resistant to treatment as well, which means that the $160,000 that my insurance company spent on a breakthrough medication and the $300,000 that it spent on chemotherapy was probably a waste of money. Sigh. Who knows? But most unsettling is the fact that it is aggressive, growing quickly. It has to come out. Pronto. In 11 days, I will have a rather radical surgery, the kind that could potentially change my life. I have been given the statistical probability of each possible outcome, and I wouldn't be heading to Vegas with those odds. I will spare you all the particulars, but let's just say that I am nervous about it. And afraid. Unfortunately, I am well acquainted with both emotions.

I have needed some time to sit with my grief as my over active imagination has played the movie reel of "what ifs." And I know that what happens in the theater of my mind is often more threatening and scary than the reality. But every once in a while I need to go to that dark place, invite the monsters for tea and cookies and ask them what their intentions are. The gorge themselves and have terrible manners. Rarely, do they tell me what I want to know.

I pray a lot. By now, I am thinking that God is tired of the incessant sound of my voice. But faith is the glue that I use to put the pieces back together after this most recent explosion. It has worked so far. I can't imagine traveling this road without it. So now, I am "nesting," getting ready for what will be a long recuperation period and subsequent treatment. I'm chasing the dust bunnies and fluffing the pillows. The cupboards are full. I continue to buy green bananas, too, because I fully intend to be around to eat them.

Count on it.

Begin with the End in Mind

When I taught high school English, I often advised my students to begin each paper with the end in mind. It took me a while to convince them that you have to know where you are going if you ever intend to get there. It made perfect organizational sense to me. It still does.

And now, when I plan a book, I pen the last few lines of the story before I even write the first. I like a proper resolution, a satisfying end, and I enjoy working toward that goal with each chapter, each twist of the plot. Somehow, thinking backwards works for me.

But life isn't a carefully designed novel; It is wildly unpredictable, filled with ambiguous circumstances. More often than not, we are stumbling into the unknown, navigating situations by the seat of our pants. Lots of cultures do well with uncertainty, but that isn't the "American way." We want to know what to expect. We like forecasts, calculations, projections. We want to know the prospects so that we can be prepared for what is to come.

Sometimes, that isn't possible. And being in the place of "not knowing" can be unsettling. I know this to be true; I have pitched a tent right in the middle of the land of random odds, surrounded by a dark and unfamiliar forest. It is easy to feel lost.

I checked the odometer on my husband's truck. We have logged close to 500 miles this week, driving from one end of Atlanta to another to jump through the pre-surgery hoops. I have met my "bonus surgeon," an impressive, no-nonsense woman who exudes competence with a sprinkling of compassion. I was so enamored with her that I nodded my head in agreement and smiled like a Cheshire cat behind my mask when she suggested a colonoscopy the day before I go under the knife; It wasn't until I got home and started counting how many days I would be on a liquid diet, that I was sorry I didn't protest a little. I did, however, ask her if she would throw in a tummy tuck while she had me on the table, but since she didn't write that on my chart, I somehow don't expect it to happen. I tried.

I have signed a ream of paperwork and given up several vials of blood. I had the dreaded COVID test, which basically feels like somebody has shoved an ice pick up your nose and into your brain. (both sides, by the way). And yes, it is as unsettling as you might imagine it to be. I also discovered that I am expected to give myself a daily shot in the belly for four weeks post-op, and I immediately looked to You Tube to learn how to do it. Now, of course, I am freaked out. Totally.

Being in the hospital during a pandemic is not ideal. Basically, you are dropped off at the door and picked up days later. I guess the medical folks missed the memo about how much the calming presence of a loved one helps with the uneasiness. Visitors are considered to be germy pariahs. I get the rationale, but that doesn't make it any easier to accept. I worry about things like locating my glasses or my phone and getting out of the bed. The simplest task becomes a mighty chore when you are incapacitated. And so, I hope to encounter kind, attentive folks on the surgical floor. Nobody likes to be dependent.

I wonder about the outcome of this surgery, designed to save me from the big, bad cancer monster. Even my two brilliant doctors can only present the possibilities. The ever-present anxiety is much like the mythical Sword of Damocles hanging over my head. Is my life hanging by a thread? It can certainly feel that way. I try not to give in to the fear monsters, to temper my moments of apprehension with hope, but they are relentless little boogers, taunting me in the quiet moments.

And so here I am, treading water in a sea of uncertainty. I am not so sure where the place of respite, the safe harbor, lies since there are so many potential spots, but then, I am reminded to focus on the destination. I close my eyes and imagine where I will be when this is all behind me, and I can consider where life will take me next. This will all be a distant memory soon, a battle tale to tell. I am counting on that.

Let's face it: God is a pretty amazing author. This is just another chapter in my story., one which has already been written. I pray for the best possible outcome. I do so love happy endings. Don't we all?

The Update: I Wasn't Prepared

I tried to be as cheerful as possible as I was led through the pre-op procedures. My stomach protested mightily. I chalked it up to nerves and the fact that I had been on a liquid diet for the three previous days. I mentally calculated how long it would be before I would actually get to eat real food again, and then tried not to laugh at the absurdity that under the circumstances, that's what occupied my mind. The nurse started the IV on the first try, in spite of my challenging veins. I think she was secretly pleased. She ceremoniously presented me with the "feel good" shot, and told me that surgery might be delayed a bit. I snuggled under the warm blanket, and watched the clock.

The anesthesiologist came in to introduce himself. He was young, and confident, the kind of man who had been blessed with the trifecta of good looks, personality, and intelligence. His parents must have been mighty proud, I imagined. He made a few jokes. I laughed a little too enthusiastically. I resisted the urge to ask him how long he had been in practice. At my age, everyone seems to be a babe in the words.

I had hoped that I would get to see heaven as I had during my previous major surgery as they whisked me away and into the bright lights of the sterile operating room. I whispered an incoherent prayer only seconds before everything faded to black and all conscious thought went with it.

And just like that, it was all over. I woke slowly, the pain ripping through my body as my mind struggled to form a coherent thought. The rest happened rather quickly. I was told to bid goodbye to my husband as they wheeled me onto the surgical floor to begin my recovery. I was in and out of consciousness for the next ten hours, the Dilaudid pump my constant companion.

For six days, I was alone, cared for by the medical folks, to whom I was simply a name on a chart. You see, in 2020, when fear of Covid permeates every aspect of society, a hospital stay is not just a physical challenge, but an emotional one as well, since you are isolated from family and friends. Major surgery is never easy, but without the support of loved ones, the social interaction, the compassionate care, it is even more difficult. Somehow, as I went through my mental checklist in preparation, I hadn't given this aspect much consideration. And it was cold, isolating, reducing the patient (me) to overt symptoms and test results. We are interdependent beings and relationships are the cushion in life that allows us to survive difficult times. When that is taken from the equation, everything changes. Everything.

I will spare you all the details of what went wrong, the sleepless nights interrupted by suited lab workers who resembled Darth Vader, the incontrollable pain, and accompanying nausea. There were detours I was forced to take on this road to getting better. And quite frankly, over three weeks later, I still have not arrived at the destination. It is a process; one I hadn't quite prepared myself for. Instead of the smooth sailing, I expected, I had to navigate my boat through some mighty rough seas. Quite frankly, I am still paddling as fast as I can. And my arms feel like lead. My Pollyanna attitude backfired on me this time.

Nevertheless, arriving home felt like a real victory until I realized that it wasn't. My progress seemed to come to a screeching halt, much to my dismay.

Recently, I have been stuck by the idea of a microcosm. When you are forced to view the world from a sick bed, everything looks differently. While your existence becomes small, confined, the rest of society seems to be living large by comparison, going through their daily routines, unchanged. It is a shift in perception, no doubt. But it can be unsettling, and truth be told, there is a bit of envy there. Normal seem quite elevated. Let's face it: regardless of what is happening to you, the planet continues to spin. It is certainly true that life goes on.

Quite frankly, most difficult moments in life are transient. The bad times don't last, and we hold tight to the promise of light at the end of the tunnel. This third battle with the cancer monster has given me pause. Suddenly, when the finish line is clearly in sight, another ten miles has been added to the race. At least that's the way it feels. I pray that I have the wherewith all to break the ribbon. That's where the celebration happens. And I hold fast to the promise that they will be joy in the morning.

And so, I look toward tomorrow. It is hard to remain optimistic. I am trying, even if that requires that I did deep.

So here is what the future holds for me.

My doctor's chemo nurse called. He recently met with the tumor board and presented my history, including my most recent pathology reports. There were slides and statistics and speculation. I imagine it to be much like those TV shows where their collective brilliant minds conjure up a heroic plan-of-action that saves the day. Let's pray that art imitates life. Ultimately, the "experts" have decided my fate: I will get "big guns" treatment, stronger than what I have had in the past. I have been warned about monumental nausea and ongoing skin issues. The friction of wearing footwear can cause blisters. (And no, the irony is not lost on me. I do so love my cute shoes) I must avoid temperature extremes, included my beloved hot showers. I will be losing my hair for the third time. I worry about my stamina as I face this yet again. I am not going to lie: I cried through most of the afternoon. I know what lies ahead, which doesn't make it any easier to accept. It is true that sometimes ignorance is bliss.

After my first treatment, I considered getting a tattoo, a phoenix with feathers ablaze as it rises from the ashes. Now, I am thinking a blue butterfly is more appropriate. (You know how much I love them anyway.) It is transformed through difficulty. And I most certainly have been. Time will tell if I am made stronger.

Keep me in your prayers, will you? God ultimately has determined my fate, and I place my trust in His mercy. Surely, His grace is sufficient.

And maybe, the third time will indeed be the charm.

The Reprieve

The past month has been a challenge as I have struggled to recover from surgery. Pain has a way of blurring the lines between day and night, with time losing its importance. I peeked over the fence into the other side, which frightened me in ways that were unsettling. At such moments, it feels like you are freefalling, tumbling, tumbling, tumbling as you hope to soon reach solid ground. But it is there that the healing begins.

I have done a lot of praying as I lay in my sickbed. I admit that I am selfish in my petitions to God, asking for a calm spirit along with a reprieve, a respite from the discomfort. But in the quiet moments, I have also learned that The Lord makes our misery matter because He allows us to understand something important as we are ripped apart. We "wake" to the suffering of others and begin to live more fully with an open heart. Somehow, we are able to truly see the fragility of the human experience, something that we all share, for certainly, Joy and sorrow unite us all. And that insight, the heightened empathy, is the gift, the prize for enduring the difficult moments. This is how transformation happens.

Ultimately, I think, we are rewarded for keeping the faith, staying the course. I certainly have been. Unexpected miracles abound.

I expected the call and when it didn't come, I held my breath. So much of my fate rests in the hands of the medical folks. I had been recommended for a clinical trial, along with the prescribed "big guns" chemo. My acceptance depended on how well my medical history aligned with their criteria. And so, when I was told that I didn't qualify based on my pathology, I exhaled. Quite frankly, it was a relief, one less decision to be made. The nurse told me that she would begin to process my paperwork for chemotherapy, which I could expect to begin in the coming weeks.

I closed my eyes, feeling the cool breeze from the window God had opened when He shut that door. The blessing was imminent. An angel tapped me on the shoulder. "Ask," the voice whispered.

"If I don't have enough measurable disease for the trial, why do I need such aggressive chemo?" I said.

"Hmmmmm....Good question," She replied. "Let me ask the doctor to call you so that you can discuss it."

Within minutes, my phone was ringing and my doctor, whom I adore, was on the other end of the line. He readily agreed that there was a viable alternative to six months of treatment and given the choice, I eagerly accepted it. So I will begin a new drug, a different parp inhibitor. It isn't without its toxicities and comes with a long list of side effects, but it isn't chemo, and I will embrace it with gratitude. I now pray that it will work to kill the remaining malignant cells and keep the cancer from returning. I count on my prayer warriors to join me.

I sometimes think we tend to place our human limits on God, who is limitless. I have been reminded of His goodness over and over again in the past three years. And as we often say, while He is never early and never late, He is always right on time. And I am learning to be still and wait.

Let There Be Paint

I am currently hunkered down in my bedroom, but it is a good thing. The painters are here, transforming my house into something new. For over a decade, I have looked at these walls, wanting to make a change, but the task seemed overwhelming. Even if I didn't personally take a brush in hand, removing pictures and moving the furniture was just too much trouble, especially since it all had to be put back in place afterwards. And then, there was the expense, something hard to budget for with mounting medical bills. But over the last few weeks of recovery, I had a pretty profound epiphany: most things we consider to be worthwhile can seem daunting, but there are rewards for the effort. More importantly, waiting for the perfect time means nothing ever gets done. I think they call that procrastination.

I have spent my days wondering how many tomorrows I am going to get, which has made each one even more precious. I am reminded of the simple yet profound line from Dead Poet's Society when Robin Williams dramatically whispers his best advice to his students: "Live boys live." I'm trying. And I am starting with paint.

Somehow through the fear and pain of this recent cancer recurrence, I got a pretty special gift, a great big dose of hope. Although I can't pinpoint why, I am suddenly more optimistic, which has allowed me to consider what might truly bring me joy, and stirred me from sleepwalking through life. (Sorry, but the English teacher in me won't let me write that I am woke. EEK!). I am decluttering, tossing the stuff that has weighed me down. The lovely scented candle that once upon a time I might have been saved for company is perfuming the air. I am reconnecting with friends. And I am inviting moments of happiness into my daily routine, even if that is something simple like a great cup of coffee accompanied by the perfect jelly donut. Most importantly, I am being kinder to myself. I deserve it.

A health crisis can be scary, but it can also be an opportunity to learn how to live. Experience will teach us some mighty important lessons if we pay attention. I realize that sometimes it is my own stubbornness, my unchangeable mindsets, that often gets in the way. A perception shift is not easy, but it sure is powerful and healing. Like the redecorating, I, too, am a work-in-progress.

As for the painting, I have traded in my dark colors, which made the house feel rather cocoon-like for something brighter. The color is called Divine White. Perhaps that's a sign. It is time to open the windows and embrace the light, for therein is the source of life. And it sure does make me smile.

What I Learned as I Recovered from Surgery

Most kids hated the predictable first day of school essay assignment, "What I did on my Summer Vacation." I was the exception. I suppose it was my first clue that writing was going to be my thing, even though it took me decades to actually try my hand at it. I have figured out that putting pen to paper can sometimes help me make sense of situations, So this will be my "what I did (and learned) as I recovered from surgery" blog. I am always eager to pass along miscellaneous tidbits of wisdom., even the foolish ones.

1. In a world adjusting to new normal, a hospital stay can be challenging and lonely. Visitors are not permitted in most medical facilities due to the 'rona, and that includes family. Of course, it certainly makes being able finally to go home even sweeter. The nurses and techs who work on those surgical wards are angels, incidentally. Their compassion makes a difference, especially now. I can't say the same about the vampires who magically appear at 2 a.m. to steal your blood. The one suited up with a black protective helmet, scared me to death. I thought he was Darth

Vader. No joke. Incidentally, If I never consume another bowl of chicken broth ever that will be fine with me. And hospital "soup" tastes like unseasoned swill. (That's being polite.) You have been duly warned.

2. Mindless TV is indeed mindless. I can't help but wonder how those "real housewives" get their false eyelashes to stay on like that? There must be a trick to it. I also don't get the incessant whining among these rich pampered women. It is like a train wreck, but I can't stop watching. And then, there is "90 Day Fiancé." I am fascinated by the choices some folks make.

3. HGTV can give you a contagious disease called "redecorating fever." And nothing happens in an hour like it does on those makeover shows, nor is it free, but change can be good for the soul. Just be sure you have fully recovered before you tackle a big project. Trust me on this.

4. The Hallmark Christmas movies start in October, which makes you want to deck the halls before Halloween. After the year we have all had, you are entitled to do as if you please, regardless of what the neighbors think.

5. Do NOT order anything from a Facebook ad, no matter how tempting it might be. Most of those positive reviews are fabricated. In a moment of temporary insanity, I fell for that cute animated toy puppy that is so life-like you would swear it was real. What I got was a flat partially-stuffed animal that

might be worth a buck or two. He sits on the shelf in my laundry room to remind me not to be so gullible

And no, you can't get a Louis Vuitton handbag bag for $29.95 either. Fortunately, I didn't fall for that.

Still, I am better at filtering these things than someone I know (cough, cough), who ordered a Gibson guitar and got a little girl's hair bow instead. I am sure the folks at the credit card company are still laughing over that one.

6. However, Amazon and Ebay sell some good stuff. And you can order at 3 a.m. if you can't sleep. The jury is still out on Wayfair.

7. Everything tastes better when somebody else has cooked it, especially after a week with no solid food. I am so grateful for my casserole-bearing friends. And then, there are the specially-delivered bakery treats. Chocolate croissants are amazing.

8. And by the way, all the weight you quickly lost from being sick will return within three hours of eating your celebratory burger and fries. That perfect number on your scale was just an illusion, but then, it could be attributed to those chocolate croissants.

9. Murphy's Law is real. Your NEW dishwasher is most likely to break when you need it most. Oh and the replacement parts come from China, which means you wait and wait and wait. Thank goodness for paper plates.

10. The dust bunnies duplicate like, well, rabbits when you are too sick to clean, and a dirty window can taunt you as you lie in bed staring at it. Try not to look.

11. If insurance denies your pricey medication, appeal it, even if it means talking on the phone with Miguel from Miami for two hours. He's actually a pretty nice guy.

12. A B12 shot is a miracle drug. I highly recommend it.

13. Drink as much water as is humanly possible. Dehydration is the source of 75% of your ailments.

14. Clean sheets are heaven. You especially appreciate them when you are too weak to change them on your own. Bonus points if they were washed with fabric softener.

15. People can be incredibly kind. Cards and flowers and texts mean so much when you are confined to your bedroom. Thoughtfulness is a lovely gift and so appreciated.

16. Don't believe the many phone calls and printed literature about the dreaded side effects of your treatment prescriptions, even if there is a skull and crossbones on the bottle. Consider yourself made of Teflon and don't let that stick. You are unique and so is your body.

17. Recovery is a process. Be patient. Give yourself some grace. And when you rejoin the living, everything will be elevated to special, even a trip to Kroger.

18. Attitude is everything; so is faith. Both will see you through most of life's trials.

The universe is always going to teach us lessons. Some may be ridiculous, while others are profound.

The key is to remain open to the possibilities, even as we stand in the storm. But don't forget your umbrella.

The Last Jar of Jelly

As summer turns into fall, the blackberry vines which punctuate our country property begin to shrivel and die. I have a love/hate relationship with these intrusive weeds. When they first emerge in the spring, I resolve to eliminate them by any means possible, but as the ground warms, the runners spread in an invisible invasion. By Mother's Day, the vines begin to sprout white flowers and my thoughts turn to the harvest. In the hottest dog days of summer, the berries appear, quickly turning from red to a deep purple. I don gloves and a long sleeve shirt as protection from the ever--present thorns, risk nasty bites from the chiggers, and make my way into the wild garden. I fill my bucket with the bounty, destined for the freezer, motivated by the promise of cobbler at Thanksgiving.

The berries always remind me of Momma. She took the picking seriously, seeking out the juiciest as she paused on occasion to pop one into her mouth. As a child, I often tagged along, whining about the heat and bugs. But she was quick to remind me that they would be transformed into something delicious. That always seemed to appease me.

The next morning, I would sit in the kitchen and watch as she retrieved the big canning pot from the top shelf of the pantry and lined up the sterilized jars like soldiers patiently waiting to be pressed into service. It was the one day a year set aside for making her special blackberry jelly.

Mom never settled on making jam, which utilized the whole fruit, including seeds. Instead, she would squeeze the berries through a clean white cheesecloth until she had extracted pure purple liquid that she would magically transform into the most amazingly sweet creation. She proudly put the jars away for special gifts and hot biscuits. If she had calculated correctly, there was enough to last until the ritual was repeated a year later.

I suppose that she somehow ended up with a few extra jars that added to the annual stockpile because when she passed away, we discovered dozens, which we saved for special occasions and holiday brunches. And each time my family and I shared Momma's blackberry jelly, we felt her presence smiling down on us. It was comforting, a brief respite from the grief of losing her. The day we opened the last jar was bittersweet as it marked the end of something so very special.

Sadly, I never learned how to make it, much to my family's dismay. Store bought never tastes as good. But every summer when the blackberries turn purple. I am reminded of how hard my momma worked to produce something wonderful for those she loved. Memories become important when the person with whom you shared those moments is gone. And while we will often define a legacy as a finite inheritance, I think it is much more than that. What still bears fruit in another's life... that is your legacy. I wonder what mine will be?

The Gift of Life

I have only given blood once. It was during one of those drives at school when the Red Cross trailer pulled into the bus parking lot and welcomed students over the age of 18 to donate. Truth be told, most were lured by the promise of free cookies and juice. Missing math class was just a bonus. The faculty was encouraged to pop in during their planning periods to participate and after watching the heart-tugging video at the most recent faculty meeting, many of us volunteered. Myself included.

What I hadn't anticipated was the backup as kids lined up for their turn in one of the three reclining chairs. Several teenagers giggled and whispered to each other, as they mentally calculated how much time they had been out of the classroom, figuring they had pulled one over on the unsuspecting administration. A couple of names were tossed around as the stories of friends who had passed out at the sight of the needle were repeated. The next day, the embellished versions would be told over slices of pizza in the cafeteria. Such is the stuff of high school legends.

I was graciously ushered to the front of the line by the Student Council member who carried a clipboard and tried to be as efficient as possible, all the while sporting a deer-in-the-headlights look. So much responsibility rested on her young shoulders, and things were quickly unraveling.

I slid into the chair and took a deep breath. The process was painless, but time-consuming, and the nurse had just removed the needle from my arm when the bell rang for the next period to begin. I grabbed my cookies and juice and climbed the three flights of stairs to my classroom. By the time I opened the door for my students, I was lightheaded and dizzy, with a queasy feeling in the pit of my stomach. I don't know how much learning took place for the rest of that afternoon, but I made a mental note to reserve such adventures for after-school hours. High school teachers need to be firing on all cylinders.

In subsequent years, the few times when I tried to donate, I was deemed unfit, either too anemic or too soon after a strong antibiotic regiment. And then, quite frankly, the idea fell off of my radar as I grew busy with the other responsibilities of life. That might be true for many of us.

But perception always changes with experience. Early in my treatment, I walked through the infusion center one morning and noticed the bright red and yellow bags hanging from random IV poles. I had quite the epiphany: for each blood product donated, there is a living, breathing recipient. And most recently, I was one of them. When this newest medication, meant to keep the cancer at bay, attacked my platelets, I found myself weak, fuzzy-brained, and covered in tiny bruises. My doctor's chemo nurse, who called with the news, told me to cloak myself in bubble wrap and go to bed. I was to get a transfusion early the next morning.

There is something sacred about the process. Unlike chemotherapy, which is mixed by the resident pharmacist, this comes from the hospital blood bank, sent through a special tube and marked to be handled with care. There is a tag attached, and before the transfusion begins, the nurses cross reference the typing for both the donor and the patient. As they call out the information to each other, I whisper a prayer for the kind soul who has given me this precious gift, one which I can never repay. The bag is hung and attached to the tube which leads to my port. While I watch the liquid enter my veins, I am fascinated by the fact that platelets are bright yellow, like the sun or the yolk of an egg or a tart lemon. I suppose that God chose a happy color for something so crucial to life.

I have needed two of these transfusions in as many weeks, and I have thought a lot about how we are wonderfully made. It is nothing short of a miracle that a part of one person can save the life of another. God designed us to be interdependent, to understand that each of us can indeed be our brother's keeper. That's nothing short of remarkable. And, I suppose, something we often forget in a society that salutes individualism.

During this time of Thanksgiving, I am grateful for many things: friends and family, of course, the heroic medical folks. I treasure moments, which someday will simply be memoires. I still appreciate chocolate and a good red wine. But on this particular holiday, I am also indebted to the generous stranger whose kindness has allowed me to rebuild my weakened body and live to fight another day.

The Greeks have several words to define love: the most powerful being agape, which means love with action, particularly when it is concerned with the greater good of another. And to so many, myself included, that's exactly what blood donation has been.

Thanksgiving Traditions

It is an annual ritual. I dust off the Friendly Village china that belonged to my mother-in-law, the autumn colors adding a festive touch to the table. I polish my mother's flatware, the sterling that she proudly collected over the years. And I put salt and pepper into the turkey shakers I bought for a song at a yard sale over two decades ago. I take inventory of the tablecloths, choosing the one that survived, unstained from last year's meal. These are more than just things: they are a legacy, a tangible scrapbook, and a reminder of holidays past when generations have gathered to enjoy the communal feast, telling tale tales around the table, cracking jokes and embellishing the family memories we all share. I lovingly prepare the prized secret recipes, my culinary inheritance, and when my grown children later remark that they taste just like Mawmaw's, I smile with pride at my success. This is Thanksgiving, the one day of the year when we all don our pilgrim hats and spend a moment reflecting on our individual and collective blessings.

Like most American households, we go around the table proudly proclaiming those things for which we are thankful. Sometimes, there are silly wisecracks, mostly out of embarrassment. The kids begrudgingly participate, joking about being grateful for the turkey and dressing and pecan pie. But once we are able to strip away the superficial layer, there are profound moments, words of kindness and appreciation for the things and people we so often take for granted. We do our best to recreate that perfect Norman Rockwell holiday, and even when we fall short, and the gravy is lumpy, it is pretty darned special. Yes, it is a cliché, but one that we embrace as a nation and as a family. And I am glad that it is one tradition that hasn't been tainted by cynicism in our modern world.

As everyone starts to grumble about the food getting cold, we have one last ritual, my husband's annual toast. "Here's to all who are here, those who have gone before us, and those who are yet to be. May we be ever thankful." My daughters-in-law eye each other and wink, wondering whose turn it might be for that wish to come true. It has happened. We often joke about the baby born nine and a half months after turkey day.

It is interesting as we sit among the bounty, reflecting on the many blessings we enjoy that this one day means so much. We are on our best behavior, with kindness and cooperation front and center. It is as though we have saved up all of the good feelings, the joy in being together, for this shared time. But wouldn't it be lovely if we could truly live each day in gratitude, demonstrating our appreciation for all that we have been given? To have been born in America, to have life choices and limitless opportunities, to have health and happiness, friends and family, is like winning the lottery. The value of these treasures is beyond measure.

As we move forward into the coming holiday season and the New Year which follows, let us be ever mindful of how fortunate we are and may we enjoy every moment of the most precious gift of all, a well-lived life. And by all means, have that extra slice of pie! Happy Thanksgiving, everybody.

This Christmas is Different

It is Christmas Eve, and I am in a bit of a panic. I have made dozens of attempts to write something which felt worthy of the holiday, but I ended up deleting one sentence after another. Most of it felt superficial and clichéd. I attributed it to a bit of writer's block, coupled with chemo brain, but in truth, I think it is more than that. This has been one of the most challenging years of my life, and I know that I am not alone. Collectively and individually, we have experienced a myriad of emotions during the past twelve months. In rapid succession, so much has changed in our world, and adapting isn't always easy. Sometimes, it feels impossible.

Each morning, the sun rises, ushering in a new day. Between dawn and nightfall so much can happen, altering life in an instant. We take the normal moments of any given twenty-four-hour period for granted, blinded to the possibilities, which is probably a good thing, but when that rhythm is altered, it can be unsettling.

Perhaps this is the year we lost the last remaining bit of our innocence. And for some of us, we replaced it with cynicism and doubt. As the pages were removed from the calendar, we bemoaned the difficult surprises and rode the wave of uncertainty, crossing our fingers with optimism. Some of us were woke and others were "shook," but we all felt something.

And then the Christmas season arrived, right on time. We have scrambled to preserve the family traditions, adjusting everything from shopping to holiday parties. We wait for the UPS truck instead of planning a day at the mall, all the while hoping that there will be money to pay for it all. We don our masks instead of our gay apparel, while being reminded that the singing of carols could also be a means of delivering a death sentence. Fa la la la la. We count the heads around the celebratory table and worry that Cousin Sue will be hurt because she was excluded this year. Everything feels different.

We try to remember that this is a time of peace on earth, goodwill to men, all the while, disappointed in our neighbors whose political views don't align with our own. There is a concern about tomorrow and the day after that because the security we felt about our nation has been shattered. Like poor Humpty Dumpty, we wonder if it can be put together again, and if so, how will it be altered? How will WE be altered?

So yeah, at this, the most wonderful time of the year, when life is normally full of comfort and joy and eggnog many of us are experiencing anxiety, grief, sadness, fear, and alienation. And in the spirit of the season, we try to push those emotions, deep inside because, after all, what would Santa do?

Perhaps this crazy year, like no other, has forced us to put aside some of the commercial trappings of Christmas, downsize the decorations, and focus on the true meaning of the holiday, the miraculous birth of Our Savior, Jesus Christ. He was the hope of the world 2,020 years ago, and He remains so today for those of us who believe.

At 3 o'clock this morning, I woke from a dream where a choir of angels was singing from Handel's *Messiah,* a gift of musical and spiritual expression written 278 years ago. If you have never heard the Christmas portion of the masterpiece, look it up. It is breathtaking. The well-known song, "For Unto us a Child is Born" somehow got on repeat play in my subconscious mind, with one line standing out among the others. "And the government shall be upon His shoulders." (Isaiah 9:6) While we recognize the failure of human solutions, grow weary of political posturing, we hold tight to those Divine words. So many of us are counting on it.

Faith is the assurance that a better tomorrow awaits. And that, my friends, is the true promise of Christmas. Believe it!

The Resolution Ritual

---※---

I cleaned out the pantry today. Okay, before you stop reading, let me explain that I am going somewhere with this. It was a monumental mindless task, one that I have put off for months. And as I examined can after can of expired beans and rock-hard spices, I had time to think about the New Year.

We all begin with a blank slate handed to us when the ball drops at midnight. We are filled with hopes to be a better version of ourselves in the twelve months to follow. It is interesting how that annual dose of optimism gives us the ambition to tackle our dreams and goals with gusto, and the faith to believe that we will succeed. There are platitudes, cutesy sayings from the internet admonishing us to reach for the stars, love with pure passion, be kind to ourselves and each other. And somehow, at the bewitching hour when the clock strikes twelve, ushering in a new year, we are confident that we can. That is, until it gets difficult.

The gyms are filled to capacity in January with people committed to getting fit; grocery stores run out of kale instead of eggnog; the shelves in the liquor stores remain stocked. Everyone seems to try a little harder to achieve something significant. But by March, much of that resolve fades as the reality sets in. Change is never easy, and old habits are tough to break. Trust me, I know. And when family and coworkers test our patience, we forget our vow to smile and let it go. Projects don't go as planned;

vacations are spoiled; tragedy knocks on our doors. So, we reach for the bag of chips and open a bottle of wine and whisper "maybe next year." Because life can't be wrapped up in a neat little package, because it is messy and sometimes, difficult, our best intentions fall by the wayside.

So as I wiped down dusty shelves, I thought of my own resolutions and my ability to persevere long enough to accomplish them, for them to become as much a part of my daily existence as brushing my teeth and feeding the dogs. Life is measured in the time we have on this earth until one day we take that big step which leads us from this mortal plane. In those final moments, we will look back on our existence and wonder if we could have been better, done more, made sensible choices and used our time wisely. Maybe resolutions help guide us so that we live without regret. It's a nice thought, isn't it?

So this year, I will

- **Be more grateful** because goodness knows, I am blessed far beyond that which I deserve. Let me be ever-mindful of the abundance that comes my way, the good things, both big and small, the kind word and thoughtful deed. And when life throws me a curve ball, may I be thankful for the lesson the universe has chosen to teach me.
- **Declutter my life**, which means tackling the hoard I keep hidden in the attic and basement. This year, I hope to finally admit that my kids are not so keen on owning Grandma's teapot collection, but somebody else might be. As I give away the things which weigh down my life, I hope I

will feel lighter, which will free me in other ways as well.
- **Go somewhere I have never been** because In my case, I think it's called a "bucket list," and it's a pretty long one, but I am hoping for a bit of respite from treatment to see what kind of adventure I can find.
- **Be a little easier on myself**, especially when life doesn't go as planned, to forgive myself when I stumble and especially when I fall. To remember that it's perfectly fine to have a pajama day, to embrace a new wrinkle or an extra pound or two. My house doesn't have to be perfect, nor am I expected to be.
- **Dance and sing more**, not just because it is darned good for the heart and soul, but because there is something healing and beautiful in the music, lifting the spirit into another world, a place with no fear or anger or stress. For me, it is the simplest and most rewarding way to escape from reality.
- **Honor that which is sacred** both within me and exists in the spiritual plane of what I believe to be true. May I be ever mindful that my existence is not accidental and that all that I do and say should be for the glory and honor of He who made me.
- **Laugh always and often** because there isn't anything better than sharing a giggle (or two). It makes even the simplest moment memorable and entertaining. Fun

is such a tiny word, but it packs a powerful punch. Gee, I love to be foolish.
- **Do something for others**, even if it isn't on a grand scale. May I be consciously aware that sometimes, the simplest acts of compassion and caring for a fellow human can make a big difference, not only in their lives, but mine as well.
- **Spend time with those I love**, the special people who understand and accept me for who I am, even when I'm not at my very best.
- **Floss daily** because if you aren't true to your teeth, they will be false to you. (sorry) Besides, my dentist recommends it.
- And finally, I have **a book to finish**, one I hope will delight the generous readers who have kindly supported me. I am indebted to each and every one of you.

Happy New Year to you all! May you find happiness, fulfillment, and peace in the months ahead.

What's Behind Us and Before Us

———— ❧ ————

Three years ago, I started making a vision board between Christmas and New Year's Day. Quite frankly, I had considered it to be part of my cancer treatment since imagining myself to be whole and healthy again had become a regular ritual. I set about cutting out motivating images, positive affirmations, and healing slogans from the magazines I had stockpiled and glued them onto a small poster board; then, I placed it in my closet where I would be sure to see it on a daily basis.

Yes, I know, it might have seemed more like a rather juvenile craft project than a form of therapy, but it gave me something encouraging to focus on at a time when it would have been far too easy to envision the negative prospects of the months ahead. At that moment, I needed rainbows and unicorns, sprinkled with fairy dust, even if I had to make it myself. And interesting enough, those boards have been rather inspiring, encouraging me to think that no dream is too big, no goal unattainable.

I look at the one I created last December with a bit of 20/20 hindsight. (That's pretty Ironic, and an appropriate pun, right?) I saw so many possibilities on the eve of this tumultuous year. I am pretty sure that you did, too. None of us could have imagined that these twelve months would feel like living in a bad movie, one with a convoluted plot. And while some of us fared better than others, all of us were affected by the threat of Covid-19 (Corona, a deadly virus with the same name as a Mexican beer). Who could have predicted that just a few months into 2020, we would be on lockdown, that tumble weed could have rolled down the middle of Main Street in Anytown, USA and nobody would have been there to witness it? Even the bright lights on Broadway were extinguished. As businesses were closed, jobs were lost, and sadly, so were people. The talking heads pointed fingers, while the nation mourned. It has been an unsettling time. And who among us might have foreseen the collective distrust, racial unrest and senseless violence, the severed relationships as folks argued over whose lives mattered the most? Who anticipated the lines drawn in the sand over philosophical and political differences, where censored social media became a battleground instead of a place to connect? I don't think any of us expected a challenging year like this one.

But quite frankly, we weren't meant to have a crystal ball view into the future, to see into tomorrow and know what is to come. That's probably a good thing, since there would always be folks hell-bent on changing things and making a big mess in the process.

Life is meant to be lived one moment at a time, and like it or not, we are supposed to accept the bad times along with the good. We tend to rage against that. Sure, we are all looking for joy, but it really is a temporary state, a place you get to visit from time to time if you are lucky. And who knows: maybe if we were always happy, it wouldn't mean as much. Sometimes, life is difficult. It just is.

This year has turned many of us into arm-folding pessimists, waiting for the other shoe to drop. It is in our nature, I suppose, that we tend to focus on what we expect to happen rather than what we want to happen. And because we have been conditioned to think the worst, that sometimes becomes a self-fulfilling prophecy. It is a terrible way to live both as individuals and as a society. Truth be told, the natural state of being human is messy, and it can't be solved like some math problem. That means that there are no right or wrong answers either. I kind of like that part.

It is interesting to watch the tide of public opinion change like the weather in spring. I have often wondered what influences those sweeping modifications in peoples' perceptions? Is there some magic formula to turn around the way we reason? Who knows? But if we want to move forward as a nation, we must. What if we created a collective shift-in-thinking? What if we considered what we wanted our world to look like instead of what we hoped to avoid? What if we craved peace and love and happiness, refusing to accept hatred and strife? What if we shed our need to be right? What if we all embraced tomorrow, confident that we might make it better than today? It could happen, of course, but is up to each of us to "be the change."

I guess I tend to become hopelessly idealistic on the eve of a brand new year. The chance to begin again when the clock strikes midnight is appealing to me. Besides, a big dose of optimism can't hurt. I keep the faith, always. There is comfort there, and I have needed it this year more than any other. Haven't we all?

We have been given the right to choose how we think and how we act and what we accept as true. I choose to believe in better days to come. Powerlessness is the opposite of hope. But like Dorothy in the *Wizard of Oz*, all we have to do it click our heels and believe. You see, we, too, had the power all along. We just have to remember that. I have held onto those old vision boards, but I think I am going to toss them. Those were yesterday's dreams, and I have new ones to imagine. I hope that you do, too. So now, I am off to pour myself a glass of wine and do a little cutting and pasting. 2021 is going to be an amazing year. I just know it!

The Law of Scarcity

---※---

Count how many rolls of toilet paper you currently have in your house, shoved into closets and cabinets. Four? Twelve? The Costco 48? Contrast that to what you might have kept on hand a year ago. Did that make you laugh a little?

Someday, we will be telling our great grandchildren about the great T.P. crisis of 2020 and the pandemic that changed the way we see the world and ourselves in it. There will be no need to embellish or create a tall tale; the truth of this experience has been scary enough.

One of the first indications that the menacing virus might potentially be a threat on our domestic shores happened when we walked into Walmart or Target and discovered empty shelves. As whispered rumors hinted that quarantine was imminent, the liquor stores got busy, too. It reminded me of living in South Louisiana and the frantic hours of hurricane prep as a threatening storm approached: bread, milk, eggs, and booze were essentials. They quickly disappeared from grocery stores. Personally, I would probably add chocolate to that list.

Inadequate resources and many demands create a sort of feeding frenzy. We scamper around, trying to make sure we get our slice of the pie, which most certainly is about to disappear from the face of the earth, leaving us standing there, hat in hands, feeling hungry and dejected…. Or worse.

In my lifetime, I have waited in fuel long lines during the oil embargo, when the talking heads warned us that gasoline, which had doubled in price overnight, would be difficult to buy as supplies ran short. A full tank suddenly felt like a triumph.

I have stood for hours in never-ending store lines for the must-have toy that appeared at the top of my kids' Christmas lists, you know, the one that was virtually impossible to find. How about arriving before dawn to wait for a place to open because the advertised sale and limited quantities were just too tempting? Black Friday, anyone?

We infer value in something that has limited availability or is promoted as being scarce. And we become obsessed with being one of the lucky ones to get it. Human beings are interesting, aren't they? Predictable, too.

And now that there is a vaccine for the Corona virus, that law of scarcity has been the cause of concern for many of us as we struggle to find availability, book an appointment. With each dead end, the anxiety and frustration grows. Trust me, I know.

Like so many programs rolled out without much forethought, it has often been a disorganized mess. Some places have had a bountiful supply. Others, like my small county, have little to offer for those who are eligible. Pharmacies that have received the vaccine and are ready to administer have been inundated. Time slots are filled for the next few months within an hour of the announcement. I try to remind myself that such a huge undertaking is bound to have problems. But then, I remember as a child patiently lining up with hundreds of others to get my sugar cube saturated with the polio vaccine. Certainly, we have made progress in how we tackle widespread immunizations since then, especially with the tech tools at our disposal.

Facebook, which has suddenly become the social media equivalent of The Hunger Games, is full of folks proudly boasting about getting their first injection. As we scroll through the posts, we become convinced that "everybody and their cousin," a common Southern phrase by the way, has won the life-saving lottery but us. Who wants to be left out, especially with talk of the next strain, even worse than the first, that has us all wanting our turn to be protected?

Of course, I, with my weakened immune system, think I should get a fast pass, like at Disney. But this isn't a ride on Space Mountain. Having a chronic illness makes me vulnerable, but not special or entitled, And to compound the dilemma, I worry if this elusive drug is even safe for somebody like me. Who knows? Even the medical folks have no definitive answers. So most days, I see-saw between ambivalence and panic. There is a growing concern in my mind as I weigh the risks of taking a vaccine, whose long term effects have not been studied in cancer patients, against the fear of contracting a virus that might do me in. It reminds me of that short story about the guy who stands in an arena and is forced to pick a door, one of which conceals a beautiful damsel and the other, a hungry tiger. It is all a crapshoot, but then, I suppose so is life.

Currently, I am on a list (I hope) to be informed if and when an adequate supply will arrive at our County Health Department and a local pharmacy. I keep in touch with the underground network of folks who whisper when the newest provider has been approved. Like hungry mice, who scurry toward the precious morsel of cheese, those appointments get gobbled up quickly.

Of course, in contrast to the law of scarcity, there is the law of abundance. I am optimistic that there will be enough to go around, and that soon we will all be able to toss our mask collection and vats of hand sanitizer. The toilet paper supply will be restored, and life will be as we once knew it. Heck, I might even plan a cruise. But until then, I am staying home and counting on herd immunity.

Fingers crossed for all of us.

Groundhog's Day

Years ago, I was forced to watch the movie *Groundhog's Day* in a graduate-level philosophy course. I hated it the first time I saw it in the theater on one of those date nights when my husband and I couldn't agree on what we wanted to see, and we settled on this one. So while the professor gushed enthusiastically about the various existential questions that the film raises, the philosophical merits of the plot, I tried not to roll my eyes. I glanced at my watch: for the next two hours, I would be stuck in a time warp with the characters as they relived the same day over and over again. I was pretty sure that I wouldn't like it any better the second time, and I was right, especially after I had to write a paper analyzing the nature of existence based on those repeated scenes. I think I made up some plausible symbolism, offered a reasonable argument, and threw in a few examples. It was not my finest work, but it was acceptable.

I hadn't thought much about that experience until recently, when I offhandedly remarked that a particular moment felt like Groundhog's Day. Everybody nodded and laughed. I suppose, in spite of my personal distaste for the story line, the movie was successful since the premise has become part of our society's common vocabulary. It is a phrase clearly understood by everyone who has heard of the movie.

But this isn't about that. This is an observation about being trapped in a situation that occurs over and over again, one which is both frustrating and frightening. For me, that's what having recurrent cancer feels like.

Last week, I offered my arm once again to be injected with nuclear dye. I followed the technician into the procedure room where I was instructed to lie on the table with my hands above my head as the PET scan tube slowly enveloped my body. I concentrated on my breathing, and I prayed. And when it was over, and I had returned to my car, I counted the number of times I had performed the ritual since my diagnosis in July of 2017. This was scan number nine.

I waited the requisite number of days before I started hounding my medical team for the results. It is much like taking any kind of high stakes test: the air becomes perfumed with feelings of impatience and anxiety, while hope dominates. In the cancer lottery, there is no potential of winning big. The payoff is sprinkled with terms like "stable" and "low uptake" or "reduced in size." To hear "no evidence of disease" is a victory, even if the reprieve from worry is temporary. I have only gotten that bit of news twice in the nine times I had gone to lie in the tube. I am now labeled chronic, whatever that means. As I considered my odds. the statistics used to calculate my probable fate, I prayed for the courage to accept whatever the outcome might be. God's grace is infinite. That much I know.

After a few rounds of telephone tag and several sleepless nights, I got the call. I held my breath as the nurse read the radiologist's report aloud line by line. While my mind is always aware of the possibilities, my heart continues to be filled with faith. My expectations were high, especially based on my energy level. I felt better. Hadn't I just spent the past two weeks cleaning out closets and cooking dinner? I took notes as she read, careful to write down the numbers of previously observed areas for comparison. When she described a place of "indeterminate thickening," I attributed it to scar tissue. After all, I had undergone major surgery just a little over four months ago. But when she paused and prefaced the next section by saying, "these findings are new from the previous scan done six months ago," my mind began to reel. I have two new, highly metabolic tumors that will require treatment. What that involves, of course, is yet to be determined, but I can make a safe guess.

Like the character stuck in the endless loop of *Groundhog's Day,* I am about to embark on an all-too-familiar course of biopsies, bloodwork, and chemotherapy. This isn't my first rodeo, as they say, and I am not anxious to get back on the bucking bronco. But I also know, that like that same character, I am about to learn something new about myself and my world. I am about to be reminded how precious moments and people are, how valuable time is and how strong I can truly be. I will embrace my days with a renewed faith, safe in the understanding that He who created the Universe watches over me. Always.

Who knows: maybe there is also such a thing as a Groundhog Day outlook, a way to view life as something to be cherished while providing each of us with an opportunity to grow. If we are lucky, we are able to understand that struggles, which often seem insurmountable, may be transformative. Those thoughts bring me comfort.

Certainly, the movie presents the cinematic version of eternal damnation, a curse that can only be broken by a true change of heart, which then results in a change of behavior. (I think Dicken's tackles the same theme in *A Christmas Carol* without the tedious repetition, but then, *The Bible* does it best. And first.) Interesting, isn't it, that we are yet to understand how that which we believe manifests itself in how we treat ourselves and others. Perhaps that's why we are destined to repeat those lessons.

You know, maybe I don't hate the movie as much as I thought I did. But chemo? Well, yeah, I do hate that.

Here we go again. Keep me in your prayers.

I Can See

I was eight when I got my first pair of glasses, after an observant teacher mentioned to my mom that I was constantly squinting as I tried to see the chalkboard. In those days, I was too young to be concerned about vanity, so having to wear the cat-eye shaped spectacles didn't hurt my ego one bit, until the inevitable playground teasing began. Like so many other myopic kids, I got the dreaded "four eyes" label while still in elementary school. And I suppose it was some time in the 5th grade that I began my love/hate relationship with wearing them. Being able to see was great, but it came at a cost.

During those formative years, I spent lazy summer afternoons at the municipal pool where my friends and I would meet to practice what we had learned at morning swimming lessons. I can remember passing through the changing room and slipping my belongings, including my glasses, into the rented locker before pinning the key to my swimsuit. As I emerged into the bright Louisiana sun, I would try to adjust my eyes, scanning the scene for my buddies. Most often, it was a blur, the sound of high-pitched laughter heightened in the absence of clear sight. I would wait for a familiar voice to call out to me or a sympathetic pal to come and take me by the hand to where the group had gathered. But that feeling of being left out, being less than everybody else, stayed with me.

By the time I entered high school, I was determined to wear contact lens, even if it was the hard type, that were miserably uncomfortable. And I refused to even own a pair of glasses, since my prescription was so bad that they resembled Coke bottles. Appearance is everything when you are 16 years old, but I think that continued to hold true as I got older and my vision further declined. "Men don't make passes at girls who wear glasses," was sometimes quoted in the fashion magazines. (Thank you, Dorothy Parker, for causing girls like me to have a complex.) Perhaps, I was forced to become likeable in other ways as a result. Who knows?

I think of the many things I have missed because of my poor eyesight, watching my babies being born among the most significant. Viewing life like Mr. Magoo (remember him?) has been incredibly frustrating through the decades. And yes, often frightening. At nine, I had my diseased, malformed appendix removed. (It might still be in a specimen jar at LSU Medical School; it was that "interesting.") As they wheeled me, alone and afraid, into the operating room, my distress was heightened by the inability to see my surroundings, to visually process what was about to happen to me. I still remember how that felt. But I have also repeated the experience through the years with knee arthroscopy and gall bladder removal.

Most recently, the round of cancer-related surgeries and procedures have taken me back to that anxious place of optical uncertainty. It never gets easy.

Over the past three years, I have had a substantial number of chemotherapy treatments and not without residual side effects. The poison which attacks the cancer cells, also damages the good ones. And the accompanying steroids causes cataracts. So my sight got even worse as I experienced contact lens issues, altered colors, hazy vision, and chronic dry eye. It was time to see a specialist.

But every cloud has a silver lining, and this has been mine. No joke.

Five days ago, I arrived for surgery on my right eye to have a special lens implanted to replace the cloudy one. The intake nurse went over my medical history. Trust me: I look pretty sick on paper, which I worried might give them pause before proceeding, but she seemed unfazed by it all. I had passed the gatekeeper and was given entrance into the inner sanctum.

The procedure itself was relatively quick and certainly painless, albeit a bit unnerving. There was bright light, followed by a rainbow of colors, which felt like a journey to some far-off nebula. When my surgeon announced that he had removed the diseased lens from my eye, I realized that I had been rendered partially blind. That part was frightening. I whispered a prayer as he inserted the new upgraded replacement, breathing a sigh of relief when it was all over.

My ophthalmologist, who is brilliant, but also professional and reserved, was not prepared for my outburst as they wheeled me into recovery. My loud voice reverberated through the quiet surgical suite, "I can see. My God, I can see," I said with all of the enthusiasm I could muster following an IV of relaxation drugs. The staff chuckled, and he blushed as he arranged for my discharge post haste.

Other than having to adhere to a crazy regiment of eye drops and forcing myself to sleep on my back, the whole thing has been easy peasy. Yesterday, I had my follow up visit, which included an eye test. Much to my surprise, I could read past the big E on the chart. In fact, I breezed through line after line of random letters. "Congratulations, "my optometrist (who is adorable, by the way) announced, "you have 20/20 vision in your right eye."

I cried tears of pure joy. This is a miracle, a life changing one, and I am incredibly grateful. So grateful. I look forward to having the other eye, which is still pretty bad, done in two weeks. And yes, I think of the many firsts that are to come, simple things like reading the clock in the middle of the night or seeing my reflection when I put on makeup. Pollen season will soon be upon us here in Georgia. This year, I won't be struggling to keep my contacts lens clean. From now on, I will be able to clearly view the world. I look forward to that, even if it is from a chemo chair.

Back in the Saddle Again

Cancer treatment is a bit like childbirth. When it is all over, you forget the pain it took to get through it. I suppose both are a celebration of life, right? So I am afraid that I forgot the details of the chemo experience after having a respite of a year and a half. Call it selective amnesia. And getting a different cocktail this time means new surprises.

I hadn't expected the huge IV bag of steroids given as premeds. The nurses always laugh at my description of getting Benadryl pumped into you, which lulls you into the most pleasant state of relaxation, a quick trip to la la land, only to have those 'roids making you willing to sell your first born for a ham sandwich, preferably with a side of cheese fries. It makes for a good two-minute comedy routine when I tell it, complete with grand hand motions. Someday, I may take my act on the road.

There is the obligatory visit from the pharmacist, who describes what kind of poison she is about to concoct for me in her secret lab and finishes with a stern warning to drink a gallon of water in the next few days to flush out the toxins, which will, incidentally, produce orange-colored urine. I can hardly wait for that show. She furrows her brow and describes the possible heart damage, and I make a mental note not to claim that. The nurse practitioner then moves in to my little cubicle to describe the potential side effects before presenting me with pages and pages of things to avoid. She casually mentions chemical burns. Really? I smile sweetly and nod my head as they talk: I have already visited Dr. Google, so I know what I am up against.

I wonder if I can adjust to lukewarm showers instead of hot bubble baths and if drinking a steamy mug of coffee will really cause mouth blisters. I'll try to remember the rinsing regiment. I think of the ridiculous number of cute sandals I own, waiting to be worn as soon as the weather gets a bit warmer. I try to imagine myself in something practical and soft that absolutely causes no rubbing of the skin. Nothing stylish like that in my current inventory. I'll also add some loose flowy dresses to my shopping list since my skinny jeans, which are getting tighter and tighter, will no longer work. Perhaps, I will become one of those glamorous women who lounges all day in a silk caftan while entertaining visitors and sipping herbal tea. But that image is tainted when I am also reminded that I will be losing my hair. I'll check Amazon for a matching turban to complete the ensemble. I have already figured that wearing a wig will be taboo since there is that friction thing. Mani and pedis are off the list, too. The last bit of vanity I have left is being smashed to bits right before my very eyes. Damn cancer. I had prided myself for "looking good for my age." That was before; this is now. And yes, it is true what they say about pride.

I was the first patient who checked in that morning and was home by mid-afternoon, thanks to an efficient nurse, who didn't play. And after a short cat nap, I got a second wind, fueled by a steroid feeding frenzy, a strange combination of nausea mixed with crazy hunger, an appetite you might expect from being marooned in the wilderness like on *Naked and Afraid*. And as I took random bites of appealing things I had grabbed from the pantry and refrigerator, Pac-man style, I fixed myself a Miralax cocktail, stirred, not shaken. I did mention side effects, right? I got in bed where I cried nonstop for a full hour, unable to maintain the dam of emotions that burst for whatever reason. And then, like a faucet that was simply turned off, I took a deep breath and stopped. My husband made the mistake of coming to check on me, and I talked his ear off until well after midnight, when he begged for me to let him get some sleep. I thought that I was being witty and entertaining, along with profoundly wise, but apparently not, and when I mentioned that this is how my girlfriends and I gab when we have our three-hour lunches, he mumbled something about being happy that I had those kind of relationships. I think that he was secretly relieved that they took some of the pressure off of him.

I tossed and turned most of the night, solved all of problems of the world, wrote this in my head, visualized being healthy, calculated how many days until it would be all over, and prayed, prayed, prayed. Those darned steroids. I am, it seems, super sensitive to them. Just my luck. And I have been on prednisone eye drops for cataract surgery four times a day for over a month. Even the optometrist was surprised when I complained about a six-pound weight gain and moon face, which I attributed to those drops. Some scholarly article confirmed it. At least I got bionic eyes out of that, so it was a fair trade. I am pretty sure that I am vibrating at some high frequency by now that only wild animals can hear. As a result, I was up far too early than I wanted to be. Maybe the super-charged nausea meds will bring me down a bit. I get three of those magic pills, one per day. I hope I don't drop one down the sink.

It isn't pleasant to be in this place once again, fighting both the side effects and the cancer at the same time. I think of all I have subjected my body to since I was diagnosed, especially over the past six months. But I am strong and my resolve hasn't waned, nor has my will to live. I seem to say "it is what it is" a lot because that's my acceptance mantra. But I also say "Thy will be done," too. I know who The Physician-In-Charge is, and I trust in His benevolent care. I have walked through this Valley several times, but never alone. And that is more comforting than anything.

My Trip to Paris

In all probability, I will never get to visit Paris. The two C's, cancer and covid, have deferred that dream, putting it at the very bottom of my bucket list, along with so many other plans. Like most people, I thought of time as an endless commodity, with days easily turning into weeks and months into years. I always imagined that tomorrow was ready and waiting for whatever adventure I might have concocted, and so I lived without a sense of urgency. I think that our human nature has programmed us to think of the infinite possibilities that lie before us, regardless of the finite reality of life. This is one of the many bits of truth that sickness has taught me.

A few months ago, I was whining about this very thing over a long lunch with friends. The women in my inner circle have graciously given me a safe space to talk about the hard stuff, to lament over what I have lost, and cry on their understanding shoulders. They listen with sympathetic ears, even when it is tedious or absurd or self-serving. Goodness knows, I can be dramatic, but that only amplifies how richly I am blessed by their patience. The ones who have stuck around, even when I am unable to come out and play, are worth their weight in gold. No joke.

You see, there are those friends who are available no matter what. They stand with you through the sunny days, and they are there to hold the umbrella when it storms. When you plaster on a smile and say that you are just fine, they know better. With uncanny clairvoyance, they know just what to do. Somehow, these women understand the highs and lows of life. And they willingly help others, especially those they love, ride the waves in the sea of life.

And so, a few weeks ago, when a couple of dear gal-pals appeared at my door wearing colorful berets, carrying baskets of wine and cheese and pastries, little did I know that I was about to be transported to Paris without even leaving home. They brought pictures and souvenirs, tasty treats to sample, all with a French theme. We sat at my kitchen table for hours, laughing and toasting, dreaming about the romantic destinations in this world. It was one of those simple, yet special moments. And it meant the world to me.

Awesome, right?

In my mind, I have always considered myself to be a giver. It is a cultural doctrine where I'm from: we are taught to help our neighbors as young children. But it is also a birthright, modeled for me by a grandpa, who grew a big garden just to give the bounty away and a mother who had elevated volunteerism to an art form. They often reminded me of how good generosity feels. But back in the day, folks used to be intrinsically communal. Not so much anymore. (And no, Facebook and Instagram don't count.) Now, people tend to step up, to galvanize, to be there for each other mostly in times of crisis. But when the emergency has passed or the effort requires a long-term commitment, they slowly fade away and return to their safe place of noninvolvement. Wouldn't it be nice if we truly understood that bringing other people joy brings us joy as well? I guess that question is rhetorical.

But certainly, in this season of my life, I am also learning how to receive, which often is more difficult. This has been a particularly hard lesson for me. It is humbling to accept help, to swallow my pride and admit that I need it. But dependence can be a lovely thing when it allows you to see the face of God through others. You see, when you receive, you understand that you are not alone. During the darkest of times, that is most reassuring because with a long-term illness, the loneliness can be ongoing and brutal. And so, my heart is filled with gratitude for those who have been thoughtful and attentive. We underestimate the power of a touch, a smile, a kind word, or a listening ear. In fact, the smallest act of caring has the potential to change a person's life, to ease pain and bring joy. It certainly has done that for me.

God sends us the people we need, when we need them. And some of those folks throw kindness around like confetti. They understand that we were meant to be interdependent, that life was designed to be a group project and that we were called to love each other in both big and small ways. May they be richly blessed, their goodness returned to them tenfold.

And now, I'm off to mix some tasteless potion, designed to boost my hydration and prevent further neuropathy. But I will be drinking it from my Paris cup. I may even wrap myself in my purple shawl, embroidered with Eiffel Towers, just for the heck of it. Both are lovely reminders of thoughtful friends, who want me to believe that there are better days to come filled with good times. And I do, I truly do.

We Wear the Mask

I could use a lower facelift, maybe a couple of Juvederm injections. I've got my father's prominent sagging jowls, and look a lot his older sister from a certain angle. Let's face it: heredity and gravity are powerful when working in tandem. And although I am pleased to still have all of my teeth at my age, I can't help but fixate on the gap that might have made me popular in Chaucer's day, but now, just means I lacked orthodontia in my younger years. I readily admit that I can be my own worst critic, but I am not alone. Isn't it funny that men rarely concern themselves about looks the way women do? Sadly, we are programmed to be self-critical from our teens when we start to commiserate with each other about hair that won't cooperate or those last ten pounds that we can't lose. I never did outgrow it.

So wearing a face mask has been an interesting experience for me. It has been kind of nice to worry only about eye make-up as I slip one on and head to the grocery store. I no longer wear foundation and blush, and after a particularly messy experience with smeared lipstick, I now skip that, too. But oddly enough, that bit of face covering has boosted my confidence. With a mask on, nobody notices the parts of my face which cause me insecurities. As far as the world can tell, I am flawless under there. Some days, I even fancy myself to be a woman of mystery, a covert spy, whose identify is hidden by a thin piece of cloth. like in those old black and white movies. What can I say? I have a rather vivid imagination.

At the beginning of the Covid pandemic, I was one of those people who kicked and screamed about wearing one. I didn't see it as a political issue or an infringement on my civil liberties; I just thought it was terribly uncomfortable. It bothered my ears and challenged my breathing. But as the virus became more threatening, I came to understand that it was a way to protect myself and others, and my attitude changed. I saw too many who became sick through casual encounters.

For me, it also became a necessity. Certainly, without one, I would not have been allowed into the many various medical facilities to meet with doctors or to receive treatment. It also got me into my favorite shopping haunts for some retail therapy. A proper mask became the golden ticket into the land of Willy Wonka without the chocolate river and lollipop lane. After a while, it even became my fashion accessory, like earrings or a scarf. I went so far as to branch out from the generic paper variety to fancy cloth ones, color coordinated with my clothes, of course. In time, I no longer minded wearing one; in fact, I kind of enjoyed it.

But what else is it hiding? Quite a bit, I think.

I like seeing people laughing, watching the goofy expressions on their faces as they tell a story or imitate their spouse or children. I like to read lips and study the whole face of people I meet. The nonverbal part of conversation can be as important as the verbal. Somehow, in a masked society, I feel like I am missing something, the chance to truly connect.

The talking heads project that by mid-summer, the Corona veil will be lifted, and we will be able to collectively exhale after holding our breath for over a year. Locked doors will open. Families will reunite and the parties will commence. Classrooms will be back to capacity. Soon, the waiting and watching will be over Life will be as it once was. And when that happens, we will all have a new appreciation for normal, the simple moments we took for granted. That includes looking into the faces of strangers.

As for me, I am still searching for a quick fix for those jowls. Facial exercises, perhaps? A better skincare routine? I have noticed that if I smile, they seem to disappear. Maybe I'll try that. And in a few months, folks will even be able to see it!

My Brave Face

Some days I feel like a donkey in the Kentucky Derby. Wish I could take credit for that catchy little slogan, but I can't. I stole it from a coffee mug in one of those cute, overpriced gift shops. But regardless of the source, it's true for most of us. We all have our bad days. And sometimes, those days can seem never-ending.

On my recent trip to the infusion center for post-chemo blood work, I had a new nurse. I immediately liked her. She seemed genuinely happy to meet me and even though our entire encounter would only span a half hour period, it was nice. She made funny comments and asked questions in addition to the obligatory health-related ones. It is always interesting to show up after someone has looked at my medical chart for the first time. They seem surprised to meet me, especially on one of my good days. On paper, I look like I have one foot in this life and one foot in the next. Thank goodness, I appear to be much less fragile in person.

So as I sat and waited on the results, she gave me the annual hospital emotional health survey to complete. This will be my fourth one, so I know the drill by now, and of course, I am always aware of the possibility that admitting how I really feel sometimes might trigger the crisis intervention folks to sweep in, Valium and a straightjacket in tow. I have heard about the funny farm; I proceed with caution.

You see, most cancer survivors don't talk about the emotional impact of the disease. They are scared to acknowledge that they are often depressed or sad or frustrated or impatient or lonely. Unfortunately, mental health challenges still carry a stigma. In a society which openly discusses most formerly taboo topics, depression is the dirty little secret that no one wants to mention in polite conversation, and so, we don our brave faces, play the inspirational role, while we smile and make jokes. It's a coping mechanism, one designed to make everyone else feel better so that they won't run in the opposite direction when they see us coming.

I tread softly with this new nurse. "It always feels like a loaded question when I am asked if I am down in the dumps," I say, " I am never quite sure how to answer. But how could I not be after being sent on an extended trip to Cancerland? This is no beach vacation. And it's kind of difficult to rank my emotional experience on a numerical scale like you do pain. Obviously, some days are better than others."

She stopped entering the data into my chart and turned to me. "You know, most people are not asked to face their own mortality in such a blatant way," she said. "Fighting this disease is hard: I see it every day. That would test anybody's emotional stability. You have to be kind to yourself."

Ding! Ding! Ding! This nurse understood. People with advanced cancer are asked to stare into the cold, steely eyes of the death dragon, envision a life that will be forever altered and accept that you cannot be the person you once were. Some things that you lose will never be recoverable; moments lost can never be remade. And it is hard not to compare yourself to others, who seem to be living the high life, one you will never have. While you feel ashamed at the envy, you can't avoid it. And sometimes, that can make you feel like you are drowning. To be scared, sick, exhausted, anxious, weepy, confused, nauseated, abandoned, and bloated, well, that tends to alter your outlook on life. So does the uncertainty.

And most of us don't do well with uncertainty. We want to know why something happens, how something works. We want to carefully plan our tomorrows. But the world isn't always black and white: there is a lot of grey in there. And some of us, through circumstances beyond our control, live here in this space between simple and hard, trying desperately to build a house on unstable ground.

My oncologist recently confirmed that every genetic test run to determine the origin of this cancer in me has come back negative. There is absolutely no reason why I got so sick except perhaps for the intangibles like stress and environment, something called spontaneous illness. And so, I am learning to feel my way around in the dark, in this place where there are no definitive answers. It has taken me a while, but I also ask why less often. That's progress.

When the universe gives us something that we can't change, it requires acceptance. And that's not just true in regards to illness. Advanced age, altered circumstances, emotional loss, complicated relationships, financial burdens, career shifts, family dynamics require us to rethink our tomorrows. We all arrive at this place in our lifetime, and like it or not, we must learn to adapt.

This much I know are sure: great pain and great hope are the polar opposites of existence. And none of us are immune from experiencing those extremes. Yet we live in a world that was redeemed many centuries ago, one which sadly still struggles to accept and embrace that certainty. Thank goodness, I understand that. Faith has been my lifeline.

And yes, the sadness monster, continues to chase me from time to time, although I have learned how to fight it. I try not to concentrate on the disappointments, whether from people or circumstance, for those are sure to come. Gratitude helps. Focusing on the good things, the small pleasures, the bountiful blessings can break the curse of sorrow. But that's an acquired skill, one I have not yet mastered.

I have also learned to accept my occasional dependence on others, to realize that I sometimes need to be cheered up (and on), to share a laugh over a bottle of wine. And that reminds me of another donkey reference. The gang in the Hundred Acre Woods made sure that Eeyore was always in tow, even on his gloomiest days. You can count on Winnie the Pooh, to enlighten us all with life lessons and bits of wisdom about how we should treat each other. The people in your life, those willing to stay the course, even when it gets hard and ugly, keep you from being being left behind, from losing your way. (And your mind.) Most definitely, they are at the top of that thankful list. The very top

And So We Meet

I am about to really date myself here, but I am willing to risk it to make a point.

I must have been twelve years old when I joined Aunt Jane's Letter Club, a regular column in the New Orleans *Times Picayune*. It was designed to connect kids who wanted to write to pen pals. I had several, mostly girls my age. They lived in various states, although a few were from England since at that stage of my life I had become quite enamored with all things British, thanks to my obsession with the Beatles. By my mid-teens, I was writing to soldiers in Vietnam, hoping to offer some support, while trying not to appear like some desperate line out of a Carol King song. Sometimes, it would take weeks, months even, for those letters to make it to their destinations, but when a response arrived, postmarked from a distant zip code, it was thrilling!

Now, of course, we expect an instantaneous cyber-connection as messages are being exchanged at lighting speed. And we write differently, too, with shorter, more concise communication, a 144-character tweet, a quick email or text punctuated with emoji's or GIFs, designed to take the place of words.

In addition to our social media pages, we seek out special interest groups to join, those that appeal to us because of common interests or concerns. I belong to the ones that sell stuff in the neighborhood or swap recipes. These have lots of members with little or no interaction, other than collective approval of some random post. The other ones, like the ovarian cancer groups, are more of a created community among those who share their stories and provide mutual support. And I have developed some close friendships with women I have gotten to know this way.

These two examples, although many decades apart, have something in common. They allow people who have never met to build a connection, to learn about each other without the distractions of an in-person encounter. There is a certain degree of suspense in that, which is why online dating is so popular, but such situations can also provide the freedom to be more authentic. The goal is to truly get to know the person and to ultimately meet in person. Being able to authentically bond through ongoing communication before actually sitting down face-to-face can be wonderful if it is open, honest and if the photographs exchanged aren't filtered or altered so much that the subjects no longer resemble themselves.

The whole idea has me thinking of life in a spiritual sense, and trust me: this isn't as big a leap as you might imagine.

My prayer life has grown exponentially since I was diagnosed with cancer. That should come as no surprise. I can't imagine how anyone gets through the challenges of this disease without faith. But unlike the televangelists, who can launch into some mighty pretty impromptu prayers, punctuated with "thees and thous," my communication with God is more like a running text with your best friend. Throughout the day, I check-in, I give thanks, I recite some Bible verse I learned as a kid. I ask for favor, not just for myself, but for friends and family, too. I try to keep in mind that The Lord isn't Santa Claus, so I refrain from rattling off my wish list, although I do slide in a request or two. Occasionally, I get distracted and go off on a tangent. He manages to follow along. It is all very informal, but that's also what makes it personal.

Sometimes, I hear an answer, a subtle whisper in my ear, a knowing deep within my soul. Sometimes, I see a tangible manifestation, like a parking spot in the good lot at the hospital. But often, He is silent, and I just feel His presence, the way a newborn senses its mother.

I know that someday, my life on this earth will be done. That's not exactly a dramatic statement since eventually, the bell tolls for all of us, but perhaps being ill has made me more aware of my mortality. Yet oddly enough, that doesn't make me sad. Most days, I feel like I am headed toward a glorious meeting with my favorite pen pal, my best cyber buddy, the one who knows everything about me, even the number of hairs on my balding head. (And loves me anyway, I might add.)

But unlike the blind date between strangers, an awkward gathering arranged from some contrived website, this encounter will be magnificent, better than anything that I could possibly plan here on our sad little planet. I will get to properly thank Him for my bountiful blessings and ask Him all of my unanswered questions. There will be laughter and tears, of that I am certain, but there will also be indescribable joy. That moment will be the culmination of a lifetime of the building of a spiritual bond, a divine friendship based on faith.

Until then, I'll keep on talking. Fortunately, He is a kind and patient companion, who always listens. I'll prattle on about my fears and joys, whisper the secrets I hold in my heart. I will go to Him when the pain is too much to bear, the sorrow unrelenting. I will share my triumphs with Him, sing the familiar songs of praise. And I will find great comfort there. You see, our relationship is dynamic: it continues to grow. And that, above all else, makes it even more special. Someday, I will understand how extraordinary it truly is.

My 4th Cancerversary

Today is my 4th cancerversary. Yes, it is a made-up word, coined to commemorate another year of survival in the ongoing battle with a fierce foe, one hell-bent on killing me. There will be no fanfare, no flowers or balloons or candlelit dinners. I've been told that alcohol and chemo don't mix, so there will be no champagne toast either. While the rest of America gears up for the Independence Day holiday, calculating how many hot dogs to toss on the grill and seeking out the best place from which to view the fireworks. I will be quietly celebrating, looking back at how far I have traveled, while recognizing the uncertain road that lies ahead. It is an interesting place to be, where gratitude and fear intersect, each vying for control of my thoughts and emotions.

The diagnosis, Stage IV Ovarian Cancer, came on a sunny summer afternoon. I knew that I was sick; I would have had to have been deaf not to hear the symphony of troubling symptoms performing a loud concert in my body. And there were overt physical changes which were hard to ignore. I had undergone six months of tests and appointments, none of which were conclusive. And yet now that I understand the nature of this disease, I recognize that the indications were typical, and sadly, misunderstood. Like so many women of a certain age, I was told that it was part of growing older, a hormonal reaction to aging. In the richest, most advanced country in the world, where hospitals and clinics with their ambient lighting and tree-laden atriums stand as a testament to medical marvels, I fell through the cracks of a system that isn't nearly as infallible as we are led to believe. That in itself was a tragedy as it has been for so many women who share this illness.

I was angry at first, but quite frankly, I can't blame the doctors: there is no diagnostic test for Ovarian Cancer, and with only a tiny fraction of the research money dedicated to women's health, it will be a long time before one is discovered. So for somebody like me, who had none of the risk factors and had always been healthy, it wasn't even a consideration. The ultimate pronouncement, along with a rather dismal prognosis, was delivered with such a matter-of-fact emotionless tone that it could have been the recitation of the specials menu at a familiar restaurant. Not everyone with a medical degree takes the elective course in empathy or is skilled in delivering bad news. And although there should be, there are no certification questions about the human condition that accompanies the physical one. I sat stone still, trying to hold back the tears while I processed the words. These are the "fight or flight" moments, although neither course of action would have given me comfort. I left the office, still in shock, wondering if my doctor of ten years had really just casually bid me goodbye and told me to "have a good 4th of July," only minutes after advising me to get my affairs in order while emphasizing that my days on this earth were limited. It's funny how the details of such life-changing moments are etched in memory.

Fortunately, I have since found a caring team of medical professionals who have guided me though the myriad of procedures that are part of the treatment process. My dance card is filled with lots of poking and prodding, but just for the heck of it, I made a quick inventory. I have endured two paracentesis drains, ten scans, a port insertion, three biopsies, two ultrasounds, three surgeries, twenty-nine chemo infusions (some more dose-dense than others), fifteen months on two different PARP inhibitors, two platelet transfusions, forty-two shots in the belly, five fancy devices, designed to boost my white blood count, three echocardiograms and a stress test. I've had mouth sores, bone pain, and peripheral neuropathy. And there have been other surprises: I developed a nasty blood clot in my jugular vein, which necessitated two years of daily blood thinners. I have had more needle sticks and medical appointments than most people have undergone in their entire lifetime. Of course, none of this is free: my provider charges are now in the millions and the copays have drained my savings like sands through the hourglass. And yes, my vanity has been tested: I have been completely bald twice and currently sport locks so thin I look like Gollum, the Hobbit. (As an aside, I think I have gone through thirty "cranial prosthetics." That's medical-speak for a wig.) But I have also taken many bumpy rides on the emotional roller coaster. I've cried buckets of tears, fallen to my knees in despair, and questioned every decision I have ever made. My heart has been broken, shattered into millions of pieces, and like Humpty Dumpty, it can't be put together again. Some days, the pain and worry feel like a permanent condition. Thankfully, I've discovered the logic-defying peace of prayer, especially on sleepless nights. Over the past 48 months, I have only shown no evidence of disease two times, and that was a short-lived bit of rejoicing. You see, the stem cells of Ovarian Cancer are resistant, often morphing into something indestructible. Recurrence is far too common. The oncology folks are among the kindest people on the planet, no joke, but even they avoid conversations about realistic expectations, fearing that they might dash any bit of hope. Instead, they use terms like chronic, which doesn't carry as sinister a connotation. The word terminal is reserved for public transportation stations.

Over the past four years, I have come to understand there are two opposite worlds in which humans reside: one is where everything is possible and life's possibilities are boundless. Here, we feel safe and understood. We make plans, resolutions and believe in the magic of amazing outcomes. Our relationships flourish and moments are filled with laughter. In this land, we see setbacks as temporary, always looking for the silver lining in every cloud. We believe in our own abilities to control our own destiny. Optimism springs eternal as we hold firmly to the belief that tomorrow will be even better than today.

However, in the other world, life is fragile, the ground upon which you stand as unstable as quick sand. You learn that you can no longer trust your body or yourself as your good health crumbles away. Instead of fun and adventure, your calendar is marked with dates for medical stuff; and life is punctuated by official reports of your condition. Your emotions are clouded by fear, sadness, anger, and yet, you are afraid to share your raw feelings because you know friends and family have grown weary of your physical and emotional neediness. Some of them simply turn away, which compounds the sense of loss. Nobody willingly accepts a ticket to this less desirable world, and although you hope the visit is only temporary, for some, it becomes a permanent home.

The two examples might be rather simplistic, but accurate. This is the difference between the place of wellness and the place of sickness. And you don't appreciate the former until through circumstance you are forced to live in the latter. That's certainly true about many of life's challenges.

At this point, I should end with an upbeat conclusion, maybe include a few inspiring bits and pieces of wisdom that I have gathered during the past four years, which have been the most difficult of my life. I could write about strength and optimism in the face of adversity. Most folks like that kind of feel-good moment. Or I could try the humorous approach, throwing in a funny story about wig shopping on Amazon, usually with surprising results or describing how to avoid looking like an alien when you have no eyebrows or hair. Perhaps I should list my top ten hints for becoming the favorite patient at the infusion center, including a recipe for cookies that the nurses are bound to love. But not today. This day is about being real and honest, to authentically honor what it means to me.

So I will leave you with these parting thoughts. We have been taught to embrace this moment, recognize the power of now, the proverbial gift of the present. Happiness is believed to be tied to how well we think things are going, the periodic progress checks becoming the report cards of a successful life. And being sick, with its consuming uncertainty, can make that determination difficult. Insecurity and self-doubt damage the optimism barometer, which tells us that everything will be just fine.

And yes, I understand that life is meant to be lived going forward, as we are cautioned not to dwell in the past. But let's face it: we all live there to a certain extent. We tell stories of our adventures and mishaps, lovingly cling to old photos, reminisce about places where we once lived or visited. What has preceded this moment becomes an integral part of who we are. So yes, looking back at the road we have traveled acknowledges the journey. And perhaps that is what this cancerversary is about for me. No doubt I have changed over the past four years because experience always has a transformative power. I am striving to be grateful for every moment of this life that God has given me. I am learning to honor the strength and resilience I didn't know I had. I am trying to be kinder to myself, especially in my weakest moments. And perhaps most importantly, I am recognizing that I truly am a survivor. It is a label that I have most certainly earned.

Tomorrow, while most folks are celebrating the 4th of July, I will be at the hospital getting a blood transfusion. That won't be as much fun, but it is life-saving. I figure that's the best cancerversary gift I could be given.

Planting Hope

A few months ago I impulsively bought a Costco-sized bag of caladiums. Although I would never consider myself a gardener, at one time I regularly planted wide swaths of them to complement the shrubbery and tucked a few among the flowers in pots on the back patio. Their colorful, variegated leaves always put on a showy performance, and to this day they are among my favorite summer plantings I had counted on feeling good enough to dig the many holes, perfectly placing them where they would thrive. And ultimately, it took me a few days as I broke the task into small segments, my energy so easily depleted. But as I finished, I felt a bit of satisfaction at completing a little project that would later bring me joy. Perhaps it was an attempt to feel normal again, to do something so commonplace.

Unlike the ready-to-grow cell packs of various annuals, a bulb presents itself as a brown, lifeless blob. But it holds the promise that in a few weeks it will wake, its roots reaching deep into the rich soil and tiny leaves will begin to peek out in search of the light of the sun. It is a pretty amazing little miracle, one most of us don't pause to recognize in our hectic world filled with so many distractions.

As I squatted, trowel in hand, I wondered how many times I had performed this particular spring ritual, impatiently waiting for the soil to warm and then carefully examining the bulbs for the bump at the top and the few wispy roots that had dried in the commercial warehouse used for overwintering them. Although I always had good intentions, I never was successful at preserving them myself since the task fell in early fall right before the first frost when my sights were set on pumpkin spice and cozy nights by the fire instead of planning for next year.

Truth be told, except for hitting the after-Christmas sales, when ornaments and gift wrap sell for 75% off, I was never good about living in the future. When my sons were small, I tried buying end-of-season marked-down clothing, guessing at the sizes they would be when the weather changed once more. Most of the time, I failed miserably, either forgetting about the stash tucked away in a closet or discovering that I had miscalculated, and a growth spurt rendered them far too tight. As the boys grew older and more particular, I gave up trying altogether and saved my money for those expensive, prized sneakers that they had to have. Sure, I made plans, but for the most part, I tried not to mortgage my todays for an undetermined tomorrow. And yet somehow, these caladiums, gave me something to anticipate as I looked at my summer calendar filled with medical appointments.

I suppose that through the years I have come to understand the great power of now, to appreciate this moment, with its certainty rather than worrying about what is to come, anticipating some abstract date, All of those cheesy poster slogans about embracing today are true. Having cancer has only reinforced that lesson since it is much too scary to ask about a prognosis, glimpse into a crystal ball to see what lies ahead. And that makes those feel-good days even more precious, elevating the most mundane errand into something special.

We have had a lot of rain here, which has helped those caladiums grow. I can see the planted pots from my kitchen and from my sick bed, which makes me happy. Of course, I missed a few spots, since some containers are empty, but I conveniently blame that on chemo brain and my random method of gardening. I think I did pretty well for somebody with a notoriously brown thumb.

I try to find some universal truth in most situations these days: being sick tends to lift the veil on the mysteries of life. We try to make it all so complicated, but it is really quite simple. Perhaps because I have been forced to stop the busy ness that keeps us all running like hamsters on a wheel, I have had time to think, to appreciate, to enjoy. I understand how priceless every moment truly is, the blessing of every breath. I think that makes me very fortunate. And even sipping a cup of coffee, while gazing out the window is an occasion. You see, I now understand the beauty in the unseen, the value of a promise, and the anticipation of a miracle. Like those ugly brown bulbs, hope springs eternal.

The Notebooks (with my apologies to Nicholas Sparks)

I've been thinking about the memories I want to preserve. In some ways, the blog, which has subsequently become this book is a scrapbook, a way to record those moments I want to remember. This is one of them.

It was touted as the world's largest yard sale, although I think that more than a slight exaggeration. But once a year, as soon as the dogwoods put on their spring show, vendors from around the Atlanta area began culling their wares from attics and basements. It was held at Stone Mountain Park, a massive multi-acre venue surrounding a granite carving of the most prominent "sons of the South," and indeed, a Southern version of Mount Rushmore.

For my family, it had become an annual pilgrimage, lured by the abundant sunshine and warm temperatures, which followed the cold winter months. The promise of some amazing find or prized treasure among the castoffs for sale was seductive, even to young boys, who ordinarily folded their arms and protested mightily over any excursion with the word "shopping" in it. But there were cool toys to be discovered, interesting boy-stuff, and they quickly learned that some other kid's broken-in baseball glove could be had for a song. After that first year, they were hooked as they too, looked forward to the annual event.

We usually made a day of it, poking around the odds and ends from the rows and rows of tables, laden with what could only be classified as junk. We would laugh at the obsolete appliances, eight track tapes, and chipped china. It was fun to unearth some strange item as we guessed its purpose. We took snack breaks under the shade of the massive trees, sharing bites of what we called "fair burgers" and chili fritos. Some years, we found real gems, rare finds, but usually it was more about the day and time we spent together than the stuff we might bring home to our already filled closets and garage.

The final year of the sale was bittersweet. It coincided with a time of transition for us, since the boys were growing up, involved in their own activities and friends, no longer eager to spend their weekends on family outings. As the day wore on and the sun began to fade, we slowly walked the path through the venue, wanting to savor those last few moments.

We reached the last booth, an impressive spread sponsored by Kroger. The man in charge proudly announced that they would be closing in thirty minutes. "Fill up a box for five dollars," he said. We looked around at the various novelties and then each other. "Find a box," I whispered to my boys. And in the blink of an eye, they disappeared. I began to pick up various items, but soon caught sight of something in my peripheral vision that made me laugh out loud. In the distance, I could see a big, really big (yes, we are talking HUGE) box bobbing down the sidewalk. There were three determined boys carrying it, and they belonged to me. We proceeded to fill it up with stuff – and notebooks- lots and lots of notebooks. "We can always use these," I said smugly, imagining all the money I could save on school supplies. We struggled to get it in the van, but proudly brought them home packing them into bundles, ready for a notebook emergency, should one ever occur. (And yes, they often did on a Sunday night, after most of the stores were closed.)

Nineteen years ago, when we moved, we schlepped the notebooks to our new house. I am not so sure that it was out of necessity as I think it was to preserve a special memory, one we often laugh about at family gatherings. And yes, thirty-six years since that spring day when the dogwoods bloomed, I am still holding on to those notebooks.

As I begin to brainstorm, jotting random notes and historical data for the plot outline of my next novel, I do so in a yellowed notebook from the stash in the basement. It brings me a strange comfort, a bit of nostalgia. The path for the new is often built on the foundation of the old, I think.

The grandkids have practiced writing their names in those books, running to retrieve the newly sharpened pencils and sitting at the kitchen table as they try to stay between the lines.

My heart swells with emotion as I witness the full circle that life sometimes shows us. And I chuckle at the memory of the best five bucks I have ever spent.

Stuck in Second Gear

Have you ever had an earworm? I'm sure that you have. It's a creepy image for the relatively common experience of having a song stuck in your head. It happens to me quite often, and most recently I've been humming the opening for the TV show, "Friends." Yes, I know, it is a strange choice, but I think there is some message in there for me especially since the line about being stuck in second gear keeps echoing in my brain.

I learned how to drive on a 4 speed Volkswagen Beetle. As I recall, the process wasn't easy, especially for a novice driver. I do believe that my momma tried to remain calm as we chugged along, the engine sputtering and dying every few blocks, like one of those cartoon cars. And even after all these years, the symbolism of the process has remained with me If you have ever performed the synchronized dance between the shift, the clutch and the brake in a car with a manual transmission, you understand the analogy in the song. As the engine strains, you must maneuver into the higher gear or you can't move forward at an acceptable speed. Somehow, you remain stuck, struggling to get anywhere, metaphorical or real, and end up being frustrated in the process.

I often feel that way about cancer treatment. Oh, I was filled with big expectations after frontline, when I naively thought that I was cured and could reclaim the life I had put on pause for eight months. I rang the victory bell in the infusion center and basked in the applause of the chemo nurses. I must admit that the recurrence took me by surprise. My hair, which had grown back thick and curly, was just starting to become acceptable and although it sounds superficial, I was not emotionally prepared to lose it all again. But I handled it, along with the awful side effects of being poisoned by chemo. I proudly rang that bell again, cautiously optimistic about my future. The subsequent pills, the pricey capsules of hope, came with their own challenges, but I was determined to soldier through the hard times, to willingly take them if they offered the possibility of keeping me well. Both regimens failed, which meant two more surgeries and yet another course of chemo. And that's where I am now, having spent the past five months being pumped yet again with toxic drugs designed to kill the malignant cells.

Yup, sometimes it feels like I'm stuck in second gear when it comes to this illness, unable to sustain remission long enough to get to where I desperately want to be.

You know, we are given the message early in life that we are limitless, that we can be anything, achieve anything if only we tap into the potential of our own minds, cultivate our many talents, exert our powerfully strong wills. The idea of reaching seemingly insurmountable goals through sheer determination is written on locker room walls and school bulletin boards from coast to coast. And while that might be true about some things, it's a falsehood when it comes to our health. Our bodies are marvelous machines of flesh and blood, with millions of cells, each with a job to do. No doubt we are the great masterpiece of Our Creator. But like most machines, our physical selves have a finite number of working hours. Breakdowns are inevitable. Sometimes, they can be fixed; sometimes, not, and no amount of positive messaging or mindful meditation can overcome the biological reality of illness that has ravaged the body. Trust me: I have tried. So I guess the shifting of gears also represents acceptance. That part is as challenging as the disease.

Truth be told, having advanced cancer is like traveling through a long tunnel. It is scary and dark, but then, far off in the distance there appears a light. You cheer, filled with anticipation as you approach the exit, but then, you see it looming ahead, another tunnel. Your heart sinks. But to walk in faith means you keep trying, even if there is the possibility of repeated heartbreak. Certainly, you pray for strength because in this war surrender is not an option.

In two days I will have my last chemo treatment, and I'm wondering if I will be filled with the same sense of relief and optimism. What happens next is still a mystery, but I'm always hopeful that it was all worth it. I'm thinking that I just might ring that victory bell once again for good measure. Third time could very well be the charm, right?

It's Been Cancelled

On the last day of February, 2018, I finished 18 grueling chemotherapy treatments. Although bald and bloated, I was filled with hope that I would be "once and done." I had logged many hours in the uncomfortable chairs at the infusion center, staring at the gong they had designated as "the exit bell." I had seen Facebook pictures of other teal sisters who had completed treatment with fanfare and applause, a festive cake and congratulatory posters. I couldn't wait to celebrate my milestone as well.

There was very little pomp and circumstance. A dear friend showed up to cheer me on and shoot a video with her phone. The frazzled nurses looked up from their charting duties to wave me goodbye. But to me, it was the commemoration of the first day of the rest of my life, and I was positively giddy with excitement.

By April, 2019, I was back in chemo, this time at a different, much more sophisticated facility, and although I was disappointed to be back in warrior mode, I was determined to win again. I began looking for the bell at my first infusion and when I didn't see one prominently displayed, I asked about it. I was told that although there was one in the radiation department, they hadn't gotten around to getting their own. Another patient, overhearing the conversation, offered to donate one, and by the time I finished my treatment in late August, there was a big brass school bell housed in a Plexiglas case at the nurses' station.

Again, I had a friend along, and armed with her professional camera, she took hundreds of candid shots, chronicling the day, including my ringing of that bell. The nurses applauded, and I gave a little speech. We celebrated with all of the enthusiasm we could muster.

Unfortunately, in March, 2021, I found myself returning to IV chemo after the oral therapy failed to keep the cancer at bay. I was disappointed, but determined. And four months later, I was done, poised to ring it once again. But this time was different; the big brass bell in the Plexiglas case had disappeared. When I asked where it had gone, I was told that they had abandoned the practice after being concerned that some folks whose treatment was ongoing and unending might be offended and saddened over witnessing the ritual. I was taken aback. Wasn't I one of those people since my condition is now considered chronic, with the probability of needing more infusions? I would never be upset if I got to share in someone's triumph. Certainly, the ringing of the bell signifies hope for all of us who fight the cancer beast. It is significant, a powerful rite-of-passage, and a celebration of survival shared by so many warriors all over the world. What had changed? And then, it occurred to me.

"So the bell ringing has been cancelled." I simply said. And suddenly, I truly understood the implications of that statement.

Cancel culture is a term that didn't exist just a few years ago, but it is alive and well in modern America. It started as a means of expressing collective displeasure, public backlash over someone or something that wasn't in the best interest of the nation or society-at-large. But it quickly evolved into a form of bullying as the vast outreach of the internet became a platform for mob intimidation. I must admit I hadn't given the whole idea much thought until now. I suppose that most of us fail to pay attention to situations until they become individually significant. And that can be dangerous.

I was taken aback. How could one person's medical victory become a reason for someone to be personally insulted? I was baffled. I couldn't imagine not cheering on a fellow cancer survivor who had reached a milestone in his or her treatment. If the opposite of love is selfishness, then, this was a prime example of that. And while it made me sad, it also made me curious about the implications of cancel culture.

If the idea behind the elimination of things that were important a brief time ago is to force us to pay attention to how we treat each other, then, why does it feel so hurtful, and divisive, ultimately causing us to take sides? How do we determine that one person's negative emotional response to a situation is more important than another's positive one? And who gets to determine what gets boycotted, muted, or erased? These are the questions that weighed heavily on my mind as I left the infusion center on what should have been a happy day.

Socrates said that if we are to get to the truth, we are to ask, discarding implausible answers until ultimately, we arrive at the one which is most valid. It is an idea that still makes sense today. It is human nature to search for reasons, to analyze and understand. For it is through that process that we are able to accept. And yet, in our present culture, where the current popular opinion must be acknowledged and agreed upon just to escape the criticism, the asking of why is discouraged.

My wise momma used to say, "just because everybody is doing something doesn't mean you should." And she was right. To blindly accept is dangerous: anyone can manipulate your thoughts with reasons that seem logical. To quote Shakespeare, "Even the devil can cite scripture for his purpose."

The inability to consider others, to forgive, discuss, and move on keeps us mad and sad. Let's face it: a wound that never heals will continue to be painful. We are relational creatures who need each other. Have we forgotten that? Somehow, we need to believe that we are all are capable of compassion and change, especially if we raise the expectations and treat others with kindness and understanding.

If we view life as something that we will never take delight in, if we are always looking for fault and blame, if we are constantly offended, we will never have peace or move on in pursuit of happiness. None of us will ever get to ring that symbolic bell of triumph. And that raises the ultimate question: why must we eliminate? To subtract means to "take away," so why can't we "add to," multiplying instead of dividing, making this a land of abundance for all of us? I wish I had the answers. As for me, I have learned that if you look for negativity, you will most certainly find it; if you look for joy, you will find that, too. Each day is a special gift and on this one, I choose joy. And by the way, I had a lovely crystal bell at home, and you had better believe that I rang the heck out of it.

The Fear Factor

I admit to watching those beautifully filmed wildlife videos on TV. I will never get to go on an exotic safari or ride a camel through the desert, so I am able to able to satisfy my sense of adventure from the comfort of my armchair.

There is always at least one scene where a lion or tiger, looking for a meal, lowers its head, ready to charge at some poor animal who takes off like a rocket. I find myself cheering for the lesser creature, hoping that what it lacks in aggression it will make up for in speed. Sometimes, that's exactly what happens as the prey manages to put a little distance between them, and the predator, tired from the pursuit, stops abruptly, panting for air. Once the threat has passed, the target stops, too, and calm is restored.

And for most creatures, that's how fear works, taking them from a non-threatening situation, propelling them into present danger, and then restoring peace until the next crisis. Only human beings manage to remain in a state of panic and distress, even without an imminent emergency, visualizing scenarios we have never experienced. Oh, how we imagine what might happen, what evil might befall us, tapping into the "what ifs" of life until we are unable to think of anything else. And that cycle only compounds the anxiety.

We all agree that this world can be a dangerous place, and we all periodically face frightening situations, some even life-threatening. Because we are able to think and reason, those moments remind us of the tenuous thread that keeps us tethered to this world. Yes, we are all mortal.

So as I sit here, 48 hours before a PET scan that determines if treatment has worked or not, I am arm–wrestling the fear. I have been in this place many times over the past four years, and the uncertainty is always unsettling. I can't help but wonder what's next, trying not to allow myself to speculate about the possible outcomes. There doesn't seem to be effective distraction, although goodness knows I have searched for one. I wish I could say that this blog will offer tried-and-true solutions for being afraid, but I've learned that there is no way to outrun the worry, no magic coping mechanism. Jelly donuts or a glass of wine won't do it, nor will positive thinking or meditation. The unknown always seems large and ominous, the waiting for the results, excruciating. And so, the uneasiness is there, settling in where it has decided it is going to remain for a while. Yes, having the ability to reflect and analyze is both a blessing and a curse when it comes to situations like this.

As I write this, I am reminded of all of the military words associated with cancer. We "fight" and are at "war" with the disease. Our team of physicians say they will use "every weapon in their arsenal" to "combat" the growth of abnormal cells as they send "orders" to the hospital for tests and treatment. And certainly, the worse possible outcome is described as "losing the battle." We are labeled as "warriors" and when we endure the worst with a smile, called "troopers." Interesting, isn't it? Soldiers are trained to be brave in the face of threatening hostilities, going into the fray without consideration of the danger. I guess cancer patients are, too, because they are left with no choice if they hope to reach a place of "peace," when the disease "retreats," even if only for a moment.

I try not to think of this high-stakes test, the one which determines my fate and outlines my future. And while I have been in this place many time before, I take comfort in knowing that I have a Divine General, one who has a mighty big shield of protection. Whisper my name when you speak to Him, will you?

Lessons from a Hummingbird

So it happened for the second time this summer. A hummingbird flew into our garage and couldn't find his way out. Bless his tiny heart. I watched in dismay as he frantically flew in circles, unable to solve his own dilemma. Both doors were open, along with one leading out to the patio: the escape route was clear, but it eluded the little fella with each frenzied pass. He landed on random objects, obviously exhausted, turning his head from side to side, surveying the scene. And then, he took off again, repeating the same flight pattern, unable to set himself free.

I started to think that maybe life is a lot like this. We are human beings who inhabit a complicated world. Inevitably, there will be difficulties. Sometimes, they are of our own design, the result of poor judgment or hasty decisions. And sometimes, they are dumped on our doorstep by others with whom we have connected our lives. Certainly, what separates us from the animals is our ability to analyze, evaluate, solve. But in weighing the options, we often overthink things, finding ourselves paralyzed and indecisive Perhaps we are blinded by our own panic. Perception, as we all know, is reality. And if we perceive the obstacles as too great, if the windowpanes through which we view life are clouded by doubt and uncertainty, we are inevitably stuck, unable to move forward in either direction. Maybe, just maybe, the answer to our problems is as simple as stopping and looking around for a solution, one which was often right there in front of us the entire time. It is something to consider, right?

And yes, the little bird eventually found its way to freedom, soaring higher than before. Let's hope we all do as well.

Lost in a Forest

I think I have used every possible metaphor to describe cancer. I tend to speak in analogies which can be a blessing or a curse, depending on my audience. But it is incredibly difficult to describe what life with this disease is like; certainly, I had no idea until fate placed me on this path.

As with so many life-altering situations, having cancer is comparable to being lost in a forest. In the beginning. it is unfamiliar and scary as the dark canopy of trees feels hostile and threatening. First, you are attacked by gnats and mosquitoes. It is uncomfortable as you swat away at the nuisances, but you are focused on finding your way out, so you view it as a slight inconvenience. But then, you clumsily kick over a hornet's nest. In spite of how fast you run, you get stung, and within minutes, it starts to hurt like the dickens. Nevertheless, you hobble down the uncertain trail because you have no choice. Soon, you encounter a fierce lion, looking at you like you are about to become a tasty snack. You remember that to escape from a lion, you must face it squarely, while retreating slowly, never turning your back on it. You fight back the best way you know how, throwing rocks and sticks at it until it retreats, and you feel safe again.

Breathing a sigh of relief, you brace yourself for whatever new peril awaits you, all the while calculating the best way to save yourself. But somehow, in your attempts to survive the inhospitable environment, you lose your way and find that somehow, through some twist of fate, you are right back where you began. You hold back the tears as you realize that all that you have endured has still not delivered you from the dangers and fears of being utterly lost. And so you struggle, digging deep for the resolve to try yet again, hoping that an alternate route will hold the key to being free once more.

Yeah, having cancer is a lot like that.

It's 4 A.M. I have many sleepless nights when such random thoughts run through my mind, so here I sit at the kitchen table typing in the dark because I want to remember this example. It seems good enough to share.

I keep notebooks of various writing prompts, scribbled snippets of ideas that may or may not become the basis for something larger. I stumbled across an earlier one a few days ago, and sat for an hour reading bits and pieces of my silly reflections. My life was simple then. Five years ago, I was thinking about travel and organizing my closets. Now, I am focused on survival.

The results of the PET scan came quickly, thanks to a kind nurse practitioner, who took pity on me when I described the agony of the wait to her. In spite of my cautious optimism, I didn't expect that I would be pronounced cured, free from further treatment. I have only heard those magical letters NED (no evidence of disease) pronounced twice in the past 4 years. And so, I rarely allow myself to think of such possibilities since it feels like a set up for disappointment. Once there is a recurrence, you are considered to be chronic, which by definition means long lasting and difficult to eradicate. It has become my least favorite word in the English language.

The specifics of my report aren't important, but the general picture is less than ideal. Thankfully, I had a partial response to chemo in some areas, which is a reason to celebrate, but there is also new growth, places where the cancer has planted itself as it begins to destroy a previously healthy area. I am experiencing a bit of discomfort in that generalized region, a constant reminder of the new alien who has taken up residence in my body. I try to focus on the victory, but like that lion, the threat is ever-present. I remind myself that I must stare it straight in the eye and not show fear.

My case will be presented once again to the tumor board. I figure that these folks must feel like they know me by now, my name appearing on their agenda over-and-over again. I wonder if I should give my oncologist a photo to attach to my folder so that they can assign a face to my medical record number. Maybe I should send them a fruit basket to enjoy while they deliberate.

And so I wait, my fate being determined by these doctors who have a wealth of experience in my kind of cancer. I was warned that more chemo was a real possibility. There is one PARP inhibitor, an obscenely expensive pill, that I have yet to try. But in my experience, that has been as physically challenging as traditional treatment.

Regardless, I am not out of the woods yet. (Pun intended)

People use words like "brave" and "strong" and "inspiring" to describe a person who is fighting this awful disease, but most of us are none of those things. Certainly, that is true for me. Like most animals who feel threatened, I am in survival mode. The difference is thanks to the advanced human brain, I can think, reason, all the while imagining dozens of scenarios of what the next chapter of my story might be. Acceptance is an ongoing task, but faith guides me. I am fully aware that in spite of it all, I am living a miracle. And every once in a while, I think about travel and organizing my closets. I remind myself that a lofty goal is often balanced by a simple one. And I've got a lot of living left to do.

Decisions, Decisions

Does a lab rat know that it's a lab rat? Does a guinea pig understand that it has a job description in addition to a specific species? Probably not. The poor hapless animals are pressed into service to test a theory or product or protocol, their lives an ongoing experiment for the greater good of mankind. Put that way, it seems rather ruthless and cruel, and I suppose that it is, but unfortunately, there is often unpleasantness associated with research and development, the casualties of progress.

But what if human beings were invited to do the same thing, to willingly participate in the testing of some new drug or treatment? Then, it becomes a choice, as the pros and cons, the possible benefits and long term side effects carefully listed in a slick brochure. This is what is known as a clinical trial, and I have been given the opportunity to see if I qualify to join.

So I here I sit, a month after my last chemo regimen has ended and two weeks after the scan showed only a partial response. I still have active cancer in my body and left untreated, it is going to quickly spread to organs that I am going to need if I want to survive. That fact tends to poke me in the middle of the night, rousing me from a deep sleep and transporting me into the Land of Worry. I am a frequent visitor there, unfortunately.

We are told that when God closes a door, He opens a window. Oh how we love to use that phrase to console the downtrodden. But I can't help but think that we have to be willing to crawl through it, not choose curtains to adorn it. And in my case, the Lord has presented me with two entrances into the great unknown. Yet somehow, I find myself shopping for the perfect draperies as I ponder what to do next. Yes, it is a metaphor, a good one to describe where I am right now.

The medical folks like to view modern health care as a partnership. Gone are the days when they decided what was best for you and wrote the prescription on a printed pad. Now, they want for you to be a participant in the decision-making process. I suppose that's to create a collaborative atmosphere, but perhaps it is also to share the responsibility when things go wrong.

And so, I have a been given a choice, a possible trial with yet unproven drugs or chemotherapy geared to my specific situation. Trust me when I say that I have spent the past few days asking the sage Dr. Google about statistics, falling down the rabbit hole of social media as I pose questions in various ovarian cancer groups. And yet, I feel no more informed than I did a week ago when my doctor proposed the idea.

That's the thing about choices: once you have picked what you think is the best one for you, all of the other possibilities evaporate, the potential they once offered, gone. The implications of that are huge, and although it may seem dramatic, in my case, it is a matter of life or death.

I am reminded of the short story, "The Lady or the Tiger?" It is probably one of the most famous allegories ever written, widely studied in schools as an example of an unsolvable problem. And just in case you need a refresher of sophomore English class, an accused man is forced as his trial to make a selection between two doors. Behind one is a hungry tiger and behind the other is a beautiful woman destined to be his wife. But his lover, the princess, learns that the woman is her bitter enemy and secretly indicates to him which he should choose. Stockton's tale of power, love, and decisions ends with this line: "And so I leave it all of you: which came out of the opened door, the lady or the tiger?"

I have no idea.

The Tears

Kids don't hide their emotions: if they are sad, they cry. Somewhere along the path into adulthood, we are taught to restrain those feelings. We tell children to hold back the tears, to be strong and brave, sending them a message that somehow it is not acceptable to express sadness. And eventually, we simply lose the ability to show how we feel, rarely allowing ourselves to be vulnerable. We worry so much about what others think of us, and if we will be perceived as weak. And so, we hold it in, smile and perform, until that becomes habit. Sooner or later, all that we have contained fills us, much like a balloon about to burst. And for some, it does.

An overfilled balloon: that's a pretty good way to describe this week for me as I was unable to hold back the dam of emotions, the pain of grief so palpable that the only way to find relief was to sob uncontrollably. I was inconsolable, overcome by feelings I was unable to process. Yes, we refer to that as the "ugly cry." Sometimes, it can be quite cathartic. And necessary.

There is so much sorrow in this world, so much cruelty against our fellow man. Even if I stay away from the news, it is hard to ignore the humanitarian crisis abroad. The possibility of an even larger conflict looms large. And there are domestic threats. Our country is divided, the social and economic challenges growing daily, the unity we once enjoyed, threatened. To complicate matters, we are still in the middle of a global pandemic. The future implications of it all are enormous and so is the concern for our very existence on this fragile planet.

I weep for our inability to find peaceful solutions to conflict, the lost optimism, and for the corruption that power often brings with it.

Hurricane Ida made landfall seven days ago, with record-breaking rain and winds. The path of the storm put it on a collision course with my hometown in Louisiana bringing life-threatening conditions to people and unimaginable damage to property. The images of the devastation are heartbreaking. It will be weeks before power is restored and even longer before the rebuilding can begin. Sadly, the place where I grew up has been altered forever as the scars of such an experience remain.

I weep for those who have lost their homes, their sense of security, those who are having to dig deep for the sheer determination to begin again.

I've spent the past week meeting with doctors and trial nurses, compiling the research statistics and necessary tumor markers of this partially experimental treatment. I've listened to tales of hope, tempered with warnings of possible life-altering, long-term side effects. I have evaluated the logistics, pros and cons to each decision, and in the end, I deferred to my gyno oncologist, who has saved my life over and over again. I trust his judgment.

So no, I will not be entering the trial. I will be back in treatment, a different kind of chemo this time, in the hopes that it will successfully stop the rapidly multiplying cells. Remission seems like an impossible and improbable dream. I am now fighting to control progression.

We tend to think of the word "options" in a positive way, its connotation implying a wealth of choices. We say, "What shall I wear today? I have options." Or "What shall I have for dinner tonight? So many options." It is one of the blessings of living in a land where limitless bounty is commonplace. But for a cancer patient, an option refers to a course of treatment, a prescribed means of attacking the disease. And there are a finite number of these. With each failed attempt, that particular medication is removed from the list and another is moved into its place. Eventually, you run out of options. And I am going through mine rather quickly.

Most people don't have to sit in the presence of their own mortality for an extended period of time. They can happily live in denial, ignoring the fact that the grim reaper eventually comes knocking for all of us. But the awareness of the impermanence of my existence is always with me, tapping me on the shoulder, a constant reminder that this illness will eventually win. That part is difficult and lonely. I am held together by faith, tightly bound by prayer.

I weep for myself, for the unrealized dreams, for the physical and emotional pain that accompanies the fight, for the realization that tomorrow isn't promised.

Sadly, we live in a culture that doesn't know how to grieve very well. But trouble will come, and we need to know how to acknowledge the accompanying heartache. We must learn to cry. And we must learn to honor those tears, to see them as a sacred cleansing. When we recognize and feel those emotions, we can somehow wash away the pain. And then, we must dry our eyes and face tomorrow. That's the God-given power of the human spirit.

Let's Have a Margarita

I've always been amazed at how certain moments become permanently etched into memory, the way the details become more than just history: they become a part of who you are. I couldn't tell you what I had for dinner last Wednesday, but I recall everything about the days that my children were born and the day my mother died. I know precisely where I was on September 11, 2001. There have been so many pivotal moments that stand out, their importance noted for one reason or another. The day that I was diagnosed is one of them.

I had spent the previous six months undergoing a battery of tests to determine what was wrong with me. I had pain and bloating and digestive issues, all of which can be rather ambiguous. But as my ever-expanding belly became a cause for alarm, I became more insistent, pushing for answers from the medical folks. It was the third of July and the clinic was decorated with American flags to commemorate the upcoming holiday. I had seen the doctor, done bloodwork and was directed to the radiology department for a CT scan. They handed me a large bottle of pineapple flavored barium and told me to go home, drink it, and return later that afternoon.

I fully expected to be told that I had a rare intestinal bug or perhaps an ulcer and that a month-long regimen of some pricey prescription would fix me right up. My husband tagged along to keep me company. We had planned to go to the grocery store afterwards, and made a list as we waited for my name to be called. I was surprised when the technician said that I was to return to my doctor's office since he had ordered expedited results. It seemed odd. Nothing happens quickly on Medical Mountain. I braced myself for what could be bad news, although I figured the worse might be a nasty liver infection or a stubborn kidney stone.

I was ushered into an exam room quickly and the doctor appeared a few minutes later. The report from which he read random excerpts was simple and straightforward: I had metastasized ovarian cancer, stage 4, based on the ACS guidelines. The rest of what he said was incomprehensible, much like a lecture from Charlie Brown's teacher. And there I sat, wondering when my heart would stop pounding in my chest, when my brain would begin to form coherent thoughts again.

I took a deep breath, walked into the reception area, and waved to my husband.

"How did it go?" he asked.

I forced a smile and shrugged. "Let's go and have a margarita before the grocery store," I said.

He laughed. "We don't often day drink. Are we celebrating?"

It was a question that hung in the air until the icy cocktails were placed in front of us. And then, I dropped the bomb as gently as I could, although I am certain that is an oxymoron. We both shed tears and tried not to speculate on the possibilities. But with each sip, the enormity of the situation grew larger and more menacing. We left the restaurant a little tipsy and very worried as we sat in silence the entire ride home. The days that followed were a blur, a whirlwind of appointments all designed to save my life. I tried to remain upbeat, all the while feeling like a scared child. I remember those days well.

And yes, I have battled this cancer monster for four long years, learning to handle the needle sticks and painful procedures, taking the bad news with the good, trying to remember to breathe on a regular basis. I have fallen into the lopsided rhythm of this new normal. So has he.

Life goes on, but it can change in an instant.

A month ago, my husband met with his new doctor, who questioned his years of unhealthy habits and didn't waste any time referring him to a heart specialist and a pulmonologist. I had been campaigning for him to change providers and was pleased that this new one was so attentive. They ordered tests and scans, including a couple of biopsies. I fully understood the implications. A few days later, I was at an appointment of my own when he called to tell me that he was going in to discuss the pathology results.

"Let me know," I said.

And I was pulling into our driveway when he did.

"Are you still out?" he asked.

"No, why?"

"I wanted you to meet me for a margarita," he said.

My heart sank as my mind went to that time when sharing a tequila concoction in the middle of the afternoon meant a way to lessen the blow of bad news.

"Is it malignant?" I asked.

"It is. Lung cancer. Stage 3, based on the size of the tumor."

I swallowed hard. I wondered how we could possibly be both caretaker and patient, how we would navigate the logistics of the many appointments, the dueling side effects of treatment. And then, I considered the fight ahead: we were going to be soldiers in the same army. I laughed at the absurdity of the thought, but I guess I am the general, and he's a private. After all, I was here first, and I know the terrain.

People often say that God doesn't give you more than you can handle. I hate that statement, the implication that a loving benevolent Father heaps misery upon His children, but knows when the threshold for tolerance has been reached. I don't believe that to be true. I do trust that He gives you the strength to pilot your way through the storms, even if He fails to calm the turbulent waters. Instead, He walks across the tempest to meet you where you are, to climb in to the boat with you and guide you on your journey. I am counting on that reassurance, the promise of faith. And now, we both are.

Lighten the Load

While I have had my moments of communing with nature, I am not much of an adventurer when it comes to the great outdoors. You won't find me scaling a mountain or paddling the wild rapids of a river. I've never been a hiker, either, but my middle son is, having spent weeks at a time exploring several sections of the Appalachian Trail. We have brought him to the trail head a few times as he began his journey and watched as he disappeared from sight, leaning heaving on his walking stick, his shoulders slightly bent from bearing the heavy weight of his backpack. It is said that about a mile into the trek, a hiker will begin to think about what he can discard to lighten the load.

It is a great metaphor for many things, isn't it?

Life comes with great joys, but since the law of opposites is always in play, it brings moments of sorrow as well. Often, it feels as though those challenges keep coming: family crises, medical emergencies, financial woes. And each time we are asked to endure the weight of worry and sadness. Somehow, we are expected to drag the ball and chain of anxiety with us as we travel the road of life. But like the experienced hiker, sometimes, we have to think about what we can toss aside if we are going to get anywhere.

My husband and I both have cancer. That's hard to write. It seems like a rather cruel irony, and quite frankly, it has taken me a few weeks to adjust to the implications of that. The logistics of coordinating appointments and procedures takes the finesse of a seasoned military strategist. And yes, I could use an assistant. I am back in treatment, hoping to keep these malignant cells in check. The last scan wasn't encouraging. My medical team and I have stopped using terms like "remission," instead hoping for "stable." Funny how expectations change. He was immediately scheduled for surgery that would remove half of his diseased lung, but wasn't able to pass the precertification physical because his uncontrolled diabetes. We are working on that. Since I am the resident dietician, I spend much of my day looking at food labels and counting sugar grams. He has become a human pin cushion, having quadrupled the prescribed insulin. We record each glucose test on a makeshift graph, hoping for a downward trend with those numbers. It reminds me of when my boys were little, and we kept a reward chart for good behavior on the refrigerator. Numbers become a way to make something objective, removing the emotional factor. But the weightiness of it all has me looking for things I can cast aside, to find ways to make it all manageable.

I'm trying.

We are taught that if we only think positively, tap into our powerful brain machine, we can control our destiny. We are encouraged to visualize, meditate, concentrate as though doing so conjures up some magical spell that wards off the bad while visualizing the good. We want to feel optimistic as we latch onto a glimmer of hope.

I just watched the first episode of this season's *Project Runway*. It presents itself as a show about fashion designers, but it is also a fascinating sociological experiment as the cast must live and work together. The gal who touted imagining herself into the winner's circle, who insisted on setting aside time for meditation prior to the first challenge was also the first to be eliminated. Were the cameras a distraction? Was it a coincidence? Maybe. But it does make you wonder. Sometimes, all the positive thinking and deep breathing in the world won't change the outcome of things, although perhaps it makes disappointments easier to bear.

We must all figure out how to navigate the difficulties of life, to figure out what will make it easier for us to adapt to that which we cannot change. And each of us is unique in what we choose to discard to lighten when load gets too heavy. As for me, I am giving up dusting and mopping. I am not pulling weeds in my garden. I refuse to scrub the shower. And yes, that was a joke, but thinking about it makes me feel better. Namaste, y'all.

Don't Leave me Behind

I don't know if there is anything more exhausting than holding the hospital vigil. Minutes feel like hours as your feet and legs become numb from just sitting and waiting and watching. I am grateful to be here because it means that my husband's surgery is behind him. Hopefully, he is on the road to recovery. We are playing tag team with sickness: this week is his turn; next week will be mine. I've been trying to use this time wisely, and I have actually started three blogs, which hopefully, I will finish one day. Truth be told, the constant interruptions make it hard to concentrate. But the wi fi here is fast, and I have spent lots of time on Pinterest. I may or may not have ordered a pair of shoes.

I've been thinking a lot about what it means to be weak and vulnerable, to have the wind knocked out of your sails. We all want to think of ourselves as invincible, and nothing reminds us that we are fragile masses of flesh and blood like being ill. I considered that idea to be something that makes us uniquely human, but perhaps it is not just exclusive to people.

My dog is an old lady. At 17, her hearing is gone and her vision is hazy. She has forgotten her potty training and now wears diapers. Occasionally, I see glimpses of her younger self, a wagging tail when I return from being away or obvious delight over a special treat. But for the most part, she is still, watching the comings and goings of the household from her favorite resting spot. She seems to have accepted her fate, the aches and pains of old age, and she never lets on that she is hurting. The only indication of her declining heath is the constant napping. Sleep is the universal escape from reality.

For pack animals, showing weakness is the kiss of death. The old, the infirm, the injured are left behind when the migration begins as the group moves to a better food source or a safer spot. Those who can't keep up during the trek slow down the process to the detriment of them all. Hiding weakness becomes a matter of survival.

And so, as I sit here listening to my husband joke with the nurses, making comments about his golf game to the doctors, I see that same biological programming at work. When you have a chronic illness, you want to be seen as still viable, worth saving. The performance, the charade is as important as the medical care. You remain cheerful, manage a smile through the pain.

You don't want to be left behind.

Sometimes, we just need proof that we still exist, that our lives still matter. We cling to the hope that difficulty is just an intermission between Act I and II of the play.

Isn't that when they serve the champagne?

In the Hospital

My husband is back in the hospital, having taken a post-surgery detour on the road to recovery. It was a gut punch for both of us, especially since he was doing so well after a lengthy stay. Here's the thing about modern medicine: we have come to expect that there is a magical cure-all for disease, a bit of extraordinary hocus pocus taking place within the sterile walls of these institutions. We assume that in the hands of a skilled doctor, the prescribed treatment is going to work. But life is not like those TV shows where a patient goes from critical to cured in a neat one-hour episode. It is messy and hard. Sometimes, the medical magic works; sometimes it doesn't. And sometimes, in an effort to reclaim normal life, we get a little overconfident. We forget about those invisible foes, those germy invaders that lurk everywhere, with the ability to bring us to our knees. It's hard to fight that which you cannot see. So yeah, here I am sitting in the surgical waiting room yet again as they go into his body once more, hoping to throw all that they have at this nasty infection.

Covid has changed so much of life as we know it. At one time, I would have had a gathering of family, maybe even a few close friends, to sit with me, offering words of support and a welcomed distraction.

But that is no longer allowed and so, I must shoulder this burden by myself just as I have throughout the past month, spending far too much time processing my thoughts as I whisper all of the pretty prayers I can. It is a deep kind of loneliness, one that is hard to describe.

The social distancing warnings are posted everywhere, discouraging connections with strangers who find themselves in a similar situation. Even small talk is viewed as threatening. And so, we occupy random seats, six feet apart, avoiding each other's gaze. It is an eerie little microcosm inhabited by zombie-like beings unable to read the mutual expressions of worry hidden behind the required masks.

Yesterday I shaved him. I think the scruffy beard made him uncomfortable. And, of course, he wanted to be surgery ready. Sometimes, something as ordinary as a clean face can be important. Normal is elevated to special in a crisis.

I am reminded of a short story I used to read with my high school sophomores. There is really no plot to dissect, no conflict between characters, it just describes a tender moment between a father, who is critically ill and a devoted son, who offers a bit of comfort through a simple act of service, shaving his dad's face. Like most literary works, there is something deeper to explore. As the father gazes out of the window he makes a simple observation about how life goes on, that the world continues to be big, even as his becomes small in the confines of that one room. It's a universal theme which we have all experienced at one time or another. Our sufferings are ours alone to bear.

Funny what you think about when stillness replaces the background noise of the world. And so I sit, waiting, looking expectantly at the status board, which tracks patients. For institutional purposes, he is simply a number. The time doesn't fly by here.

At this hospital, when a baby is born, the muzak is replaced by a few melodious bars of "Lullaby and Good Night." For a moment, everyone stops and smiles as they silently welcome a new life into this world. It really is lovely. I've tried to count how many tiny new souls have joined us in the three hours that I have been sitting here -at least 4.

But I have also witnessed a woman sit quietly with the hospital representative who had come to console her after she had been told of her loved ones passing. He was warm and professional as he handed her the clipboard of requisite paperwork to sign. I could only imagine her grief, compounded, no doubt, by the fact that she had to face it alone. It was heartbreaking.

This place certainly represents the bookends of life, birth and death. It's a small world, one filled with both joy and sorrow. And I can't wait to get out of here.

The Science of Writing

You have probably heard math whizzes brag about the prowess of their highly developed left brains, while the imaginative types, claim to be right brained, touting their creativity as irrefutable evidence. And yes, the left brain, the digital brain, controls reading and analyzing, calculation, and logical thinking, while the right brain, the analog brain, controls three-dimensional sense, creativity, and artistic expression. The way I see it, there is no greater activity that forces both sides of the brain to work harmoniously, communicating with each other in a simultaneous dance of firing synapses, than writing. That makes it pretty awesome… and difficult.

We often refer to writing as a creative process, an inventive endeavor, heavily imbedded in the imaginings of the author, a land filled with unicorns and rainbows. But it is so much more than that. It is a science as well. Why? Because, like science, writing is an act of discovery…. of ourselves, our characters, and our world. Penning a story is much like going on an archeological expedition, as we excavate the layers in search of something meaningful and important. And with each swing of the metaphorical pick and ax, every dig of the shovel, we learn something new, something exciting. There is a wonderment that accompanies that discovery.

So the writer pens a draft, conceives a story. And like biology, the ultimate science, where a cell multiplies and becomes a living thing, there is a gestational period, where the idea is nurtured. In fact, the greatest scientific discoveries are born of a stubborn persistence, an idea that may seem impossible if not improbable. And then, you care for it, suffer for it, worry about it, all the while hoping that the vision will come a reality. As you burn the midnight oil, it grows and develops, until it is ready to be ushered into the world, hopefully to make a difference. Sounds like an ideal way to describe a book, too, doesn't it?

When we think of scientific thought, we picture complicated experiments, with Bunsen burners blasting at full speed, beakers filled with a bubbling brew. It is goal-directed, outcome based. But so is writing (minus the fancy equipment.) Scientists observe, look for clues. So do writers. And then, the experiment begins, as both the writer and the scientist set out to determine if the evidence points to a truth, if reasoning leads to a conclusion based on that observation.

And sometimes the experiment fails. The story falls flat. The idea you have nursed to a logical conclusion is hopelessly flawed, and you are left with no choice but to pick yourself up and try again, employ a different approach. Yes, science is logical, precise.

One drop of a reactive compound can be disaster in an unstable environment. But a good story can also be doomed it is doesn't flow smoothly. And obsessing over the syntax, the exact word choice or proper placement of a comma is, well, downright scientific.

Ultimately, in both science and writing there is an overwhelming desire to understand our world – to explore, to fail, to hope, and ultimately, to dream. It's an idea that is quite exciting, isn't it?

Embracing the New Year

This afternoon, on the eve of New Year's Eve, I have been sitting here trying to think of how to close the books on the old year, while embracing that which is to come with hope and optimism. Quite frankly, I am stumped. Somehow, the usual clever slogans don't seem quite appropriate.

We are told that to everything there is a season and purpose. Sometimes, we have to wonder what the reason for some circumstances might be, and often, that isn't made clear to us. The mystery that surrounds hard times remains. Yet as one experience gives way to another, we wonder what surprises await us, and we anticipate happy moments. At the end of December, we look ahead, set lofty goals for ourselves as we turn the page on the calendar. The blank slate, which brings out the best in us, is ripe with possibilities. It's a new beginning, a chance to transform into an improved version of ourselves. And honestly, there is something magical about the expectation of a better tomorrow. For most of us, we can't wait to get started.

But first, we must bid goodbye to the old. The end of the year is the punctuation of the experiences of the previous 365 days. It is the period at the end of the sentence, the final chapter before starting a new story. It's a time to be a little retrospective, to celebrate our successes, to count our blessings, to wonder what we have learned. We hold tightly to the memories of good times while trying not to think about the challenges. But in the scorecard of life, the past twelve months have been tough for many of us, including me.

So how can I put a positive spin on a genuinely difficult year?

Two words: I survived. (and so did you)

Here in the South, we cook black eyed peas and greens on January 1st for good luck and money. While I don't consider myself to be particularly superstitious, I'll be bringing out the sage, horseshoes and four-leaf clovers. It can't hurt. I will also whisper a little prayer at midnight. I hope you will, too.

Happy New Year, everybody. May the coming days be joyful ones.

It's a Snow Day

Two days ago, I stood in the checkout line at the grocery store for twenty minutes. It was unusual, since mine prides itself on stellar customer service. They even take your bags to the car for you with a smile and a "Have a good day." But like so many people, I was compelled to stock up for the approaching weather, a ritual akin to those busy squirrels gathering nuts in the winter. As I waited my turn to put my food on the conveyor belt, I wondered how many times I had done this. When I lived in South Louisiana, buying bread and milk, along with the appropriate adult beverages, seemed as normal as breathing when tropical storms and possible hurricanes threatened all too often in the fall. And that could be a little unsettling. But the snow forecast is a little different, a rare occurrence in Georgia, and we embrace it with the same kind of excitement as we do Santa's visit on Christmas morning.

Everything shuts down here before the first flake hits the ground. Our roads are not made for icy travel. We lack the equipment or the manpower to clear things quickly, so a snow day is a license to just be, permission to suspend the work and responsibilities that plague us on a daily basis. We get to watch old movies as we hunker down under the blankets and stoke the fireplace. Families gather near, enjoying the togetherness that our busy life often prevents us from enjoying. The calories in junk food don't count on such a day, so we open that bag of chips, heat up the cocoa and eat the cookies. It just tastes better as we gaze out the windows at the spectacle, the winter wonderland that Mother Nature has so graciously delivered. It is a gift, all wrapped in white.

At some point, we all don our long underwear, our heaviest coats and gloves and go out to explore. We take pictures to document the occasion, to share years later. Garbage can lids are pressed into service as makeshift sleds. And although we rarely get more than an inch or two, we scoop and sweep, giving life to the three-ball wonder we call a snowman. Indeed, there is nothing like the allure of snow in the South to turn even the oldest member of the group into a kid again, throwing handfuls of the white powder at each other with wild abandon.

Yeah, it is quite spectacular. And so this morning, much to my delight, I woke to a soft white blanket covering everything. The landscape sparkled, glistening in the sun, its brightness reflecting off of the rooftops and trees. It is all so lovely, a calm stillness in the air. And I stood at the window in awe, just taking it all in, trying to make a memory I can later recall.

People who have moved here from the North, often shake their heads in confusion over our fascination with the stuff. They have lived with it, plowed through it and simply regard it as a meteorological nuisance. But for those of us who say "y'all" on a regular basis, it is pretty darned special.

And now, if you will excuse me, I have to go check the brownies I just put in the oven. My New Year's Resolution to diet is being deferred. After all, it is a snow day.

Remembering Lola

We were foster failures. Normally, labeling any endeavor as a failure would be considered a disappointment, but in the topsy-turvy world of saving animals, it is a triumph. And in our case, it didn't take us long to realize that although we had offered Lola a temporary home, she had stolen our hearts so quickly and completely that we couldn't possibly imagine letting her go.

We met her one sunny August afternoon after we had been contacted by a Bijon rescue group in desperate need of a family willing to keep her for a few weeks. They had found her in deplorable conditions, filthy and hungry, living in a puppy mill, the kind where innocent animals are viewed as money-making machines until they can no longer reproduce. It is a painful existence for them, and she was among the nameless souls who had never experienced affection or received proper care. After hearing her heartbreaking story, of course, we wanted to help.

I sat on the floor to greet her as she entered our house, tail tucked under, looking confused in this new environment. Her hips were unusually wide, and her belly hung low, swaying as she walked, a remnant of her days as a breeder. I spoke softly to her, trying to give her a moment to understand that she was safe, but as I reached out to pet her, she flinched. It broke my heart. But she was no shrinking violet. Once she spied my husband, she snarled, showing him every one of her pretty little teeth as though somehow, she fully intended to defend herself against this much-larger enemy. We determined that she had probably been abused at the hands of a male keeper, which made her distrustful of all men. Their relationship would take time. But within the hour, she had crept closer to me, curled up a few inches from where I sat and closed her eyes. She had chosen: I was to be her person.

We soon discovered that she had no idea how to live in a house or among people. She had no potty training and the first time we took her out into the grass, she stood cold still as though unsure of what to do. Our other Bijon, Boudreaux, tried to engage her in play, but without proper socialization, she simply didn't know how to be a dog.

Those first days with us were challenging, but we were determined to help her understand that she was free, that no harm would come to her under our watch. And by the end of the first week, she was following me through the house and sleeping on the floor on my side of the bed. And when it was determined that she was ready to be adopted, we knew that she was ours.

I wish I could tell you that from that moment on, she became the best dog ever, but there were difficulties. She snipped at any male she encountered, even young boys. We learned to keep her away when a repairman showed up or kids came to visit. She became territorial when it came to things like food and later, obsessed with a third rescue Bijon that we added to the family, who became the object of both her affection and her frustration. She had issues, no doubt, but I couldn't help but admire her indomitable spirit, her strength and determination to survive, even though the odds were overwhelmingly against her. In spite of being occasionally problematic, she was my girl, and I adored her.

But time is a great healer, and age mellowed her. After a while, she no longer felt the need to fight or protect herself. And although it took her a long time to realize that she was safe with both of us, when she did, it was as though a light switch went off in her little head, and she became the most loyal, affectionate dog ever.

She was my muse: I wrote 4 novels with her curled up at my feet. She was my nurse: through every surgery and chemo treatment, she stayed by my side offering comfort and companionship. She was my sidekick: With every step I took, she was right behind me. Her devotion to me was undeniable. We were a team, and she knew it.

I am convinced that one of the great tragedies of this life is that comparatively, our furry companions are only here for a short period of time. Perhaps that's why they must pack so much into each moment. Undoubtedly, it is hard to watch your dog get old and tired and achy. But they have an uncanny way of letting you know when it is time, when their bodies begin to fail. And because you have promised a lifetime of devoted care, you must let them go, even though the pain of facing that loss is unbearable.

Lola was 17; that's 119 in human years. She was almost blind and totally deaf. No longer able to do what she once could, she slept most of the day and accepted wearing diapers through the night. But the week before Christmas, something changed. She had been out of sorts for a while, struggling to walk, refusing to eat, even her favorite food (which was chicken, by the way). After several days of witnessing her distress, seeing the pain in her eyes, I made the gut-wrenching decision to let her go. Although I selfishly wanted to keep her with me, I knew I couldn't allow her to suffer. This was to be my final act of love for her. My heart broke as I held her tight, whispering in her ear as I said goodbye. It was over in a matter of minutes, a peaceful transition from this life into the next. She showed me how to live; she showed me how to die.

It is great mystery to me how dogs can bond so readily with humans, how they trust, even after people have let them down through neglect or abuse. They don't hold grudges and are quick to forgive, to willingly start over again. They simply want to love and be loved in return. Dogs live honest, brave, beautiful lives, unafraid of what tomorrow might bring. We could learn a lot from them.

Lola brought me great affection, joy, and laughter, leaving an indelible paw print on my heart. She never learned fancy tricks, nor did she carry an impressive pedigree, but she didn't need to. She was perfect just as she was, my once-in-a lifetime dog, and I am going to miss her for the rest of my days. You know, I thought that I was saving her all those many years ago, but in reality, she saved me. And for that, I am mighty grateful.

The Five Stages of Cancer

We are all familiar with the five stages of grief that begins with denial and ends with acceptance. Like most of the truly difficult moments in life, it is a long emotional transformation. Mourning can come as a result of divorce, job-loss, illness. Even the end of a dream can trigger those feelings of sadness. Most of us have experienced these steps as a response to the ongoing Covid pandemic: at first, we thought it was an exaggerated ailment, inconvenient like the flu, but as statistics and experience proved that the threat is real, we have moved to what we now call the "new normal."

Having cancer means going through a similar process.

It begins with a life-changing diagnosis. Sometimes, being able to attach a label to the troubling physical symptoms can be a relief, but most often it is shocking, unleashing a tidal wave of anxiety. Suddenly, you are aware of your own mortality as you are given a stage and survival statistics. You begin to wonder how much of your life remains. This is a frightening place to be.

But most cancer patients are quickly plunged into treatment, the second stage, which may or may not also involve surgery. Depending on the type and frequency of chemotherapy or radiation, the focus here is on managing side effects, which can be debilitating at times. If all goes well, it works, and the end result is remission or no evidence of disease.

Lots of folks remain here for years, or sometimes forever, having defeated the beast and reclaimed their lives. They are the lucky ones.

Unfortunately, for many, the cancer returns. This is the chronic stage. Here, treatment becomes a way of life, with medical appointments occupying much of your social calendar. Although not impossible, at this point, there is little hope for a cure as the goal is to simply manage the disease, to keep those nasty little malignant cells from finding their way to other parts of the body.

But cancer is crafty. Sometimes, it figures out a way around the medicine designed to contain it, developing a resistance as it begins to grow, metastasizing. Most oncologists call this progression. At this point, they throw whatever is available in their medical arsenal to contain the damage, with stability as the ultimate goal.

And when all of the available options fail, hospice is recommended. Here the emotional, spiritual, and physical needs are addressed as the patient is gently cared for in the transition from this life into the next.

The idea of stages has been weighing heavily on my mind. In the four years since diagnosis I have been through so many therapeutic measures, I often wonder how many remain. It is kind of like eating at your favorite restaurant every day for a year. Eventually, you will have tried everything on the menu. Then what? It's a scary question with ambiguous answers.

And the past month has meant big changes for me as my gyno oncologist has decided to change to a surgery-only practice, and I have moved my care into the hands of a new doctor, one who is incredibly skilled and kind, but with whom I have no history. Those connections are vital. But I have high hopes that this will be a good change on many levels. I'm already seeing some impressive differences.

So yesterday, I had my second visit with her, this time to review the results of my recent PET scan to determine if I am to continue with my current treatment. I was optimistic, hopeful that this newest combination would be the magic formula to keep me stable.

The news was disappointing. I was at the chronic stage, but now I have progression. Cancer has spread to my lungs and is dancing around my liver. The tumor in the presacral space has doubled in size and become highly active. Two of my lymph nodes are positive. I think they call this a kick-in-the-gut moment. As irrational as it may be, I can't help but feel like a failure, disappointed in my body's inability to overcome this thing.

I was brave. I listened attentively to the treatment plan I am to begin as soon as insurance agrees to pay for it. I nodded in understanding and thanked everyone for their efforts to save me. But when I got to my car I cried, and then I called a friend and cried some more. It is easy to revert back to that denial stage at such moments, to speculate on medical errors or to rationalize that you have enough strength to continue the fight. The survival instinct is strong. I also think it is human nature to want to be optimistic, even when circumstances prove otherwise.

And I am.

When you have cancer, you become a quick study in medical terminology and procedures. You spend your free time researching and wondering. But you also spend it praying, reserving some quiet time with The Almighty, in whose hands your future rests. Faith grows in this uncertain soil. But let's face it: none of us get out of this life alive, in spite of what we might think. We all have that return ticket home with an undisclosed date and time stamped on it. God is the conductor of this train.

Until then, I will embrace each moment, live with a sense of urgency, seek new adventures, do what brings me joy. I will spend time with those who mean so much to me and remember to laugh at the absurdity of life. I will try to be productive, to consistently work on this new novel I recently started. And I will pray that I will be able to accept whatever comes along because it is there that peace dwells.

Chasing Waterfalls

I felt the perception shift like a seismic rumble, the effect so powerful that it rattled my bones. That description might be a little too dramatic, even for me, but I can say that I woke suddenly at 3 a.m. shortly after starting this new treatment, the one that is kicking my butt into next week, with a renewed sense of urgency about my life. When you spend your days battling the laundry list of side effects from chemotherapy (and I will spare you the details here), you tend to look at life differently. The sands are running through the hourglass faster than I'd like, and I no longer have the luxury of time to wait until tomorrow or next Thursday to do what makes me happy. I tell you all this because it is one of the most important lessons that having cancer has taught me. I don't want for you to wait for some life-altering event for you to figure this out. You're welcome.

I seem to spend much of my time with the medical folks, my dance card filled with various appointments. This is my seventh different kind of treatment, the seventh time I have signed the permission-to-treat form, along with the one that describes the potential harm that might happen as a result. The Bible is rife with positive references to the number, which symbolizes completeness. So is Vegas, but I digress. I take it as a sign that lucky number seven will bring this cancer monster to its knees.

But I have to get through it first. I rest more than I would like to, saving my energy for important things like cleaning the house. (That was meant to be sarcastic.) It is easy to fall into the rhythm that sickness demands, the all-too-familiar tune playing continuously as I dance along. It has been over four years. I know the steps all too well.

I often wonder what's going on in the world, trying not to be envious of the big fun that I imagine everybody else is having. Isn't it funny how at pivotal moments we are once again kids on a playground, hoping that we get a turn on the merry-go-round? I don't' want to be the one sidelined, watching the action from afar. Like The Little Mermaid, I want to be where the people are. It's time to adjust my sails and focus on what brings me joy.

The bucket that holds my proverbial list is more like a small pail, the realities of my current situation keeping me tethered to home. But what about a shorter trip? I have 6 days of freedom before I start the next round of treatment. That's 144 hours filled with potential.

I want to eat a big stack of pancakes from the cheesiest tourist restaurant I can find. I want to go high into the mountains and see the beauty that God created. I want to be removed from the distractions and busy-ness of life, even if for just a moment. I need to disconnect and reconnect. Yeah, I even want to go chasing waterfalls. (My regards to TLC.) I've got lofty plans, although I will probably just enjoy the scenery from the passenger's seat of the car. Fine with me; it beats being in a sickbed.

So here I sit, writing this while in the infusion center, a bright yellow bag of platelets being pumped into my body. It was a non-negotiable from my medical team after yesterday's bloodwork proved me unfit for travel (and handling sharp objects.) But tomorrow, I will be on my way to the Smoky Mountains for a few days, and I am as excited as a kid on Christmas Eve.

And that 3 a.m. wake up? It was to the sound of Kelly Clarkston singing "What doesn't kill you makes you stronger." Chemo had not yet been discovered when Nietzsche penned the aphorism, unaware that someday it would be set to music, but it is the perfect theme song for cancer patients everywhere. I am stronger, and wiser, I might add, although some days I am convinced that treatment is trying to hasten my demise.

I concentrate on beating this thing, I promise myself to plan a few well-needed getaways. My soul must be recharged if my body is going to be strong enough to fight. As for now I see Tennessee bar-b-que in my future, and I will enjoy every bite, even if I have to chase it with anti-nausea meds. Life is for living, my friends, and today is the first day of the rest of my life.

Love Thyself

I spend a lot of time in the infusion center hooked up to some drug designed to kill this cancer and keep me on my feet. This week, I racked up over twelve hours here, and crazy as it sounds, when I get in my car, my phone tells me that I will be at the hospital in thirty minutes with typical traffic. I do believe that A.I. thinks I work here. I try to imagine it as my day at the spa, but I'm just kidding myself since they don't offer massages or pedicures. It does, however, give me a big block of time to write, to think about what's important enough to share. Here is the latest:

The Bible is filled with instructions, rules by which we are expected to live, and most make absolute sense. Certainly, in order to have a safe and orderly society in which to live, we can't steal or kill or lie or covet. God covered all of those important bases in the "Big Ten." But when Jesus was asked to reveal the Greatest Commandment, the one which was to become the foundation for Christianity, his reply was simple: "You are to love God with all of your heart, soul, and mind." And He quickly followed with the second, "And love your neighbor as yourself." These instructions appear in the Old Testament as well. In my mind, that makes them pretty important.

I'm no Biblical scholar, but I don't think a person has to be one in order to walk with God. But for me, thinking about the deeper implications of a particular verse makes it more personal. And for some reason, I have been considering this one a lot lately.

The first part is the obvious foundation of faith. Placing God first in your life is the essential step toward conversion, and living it on a daily basis allows for spiritual growth and a personal relationship with the Father. But I think the second one is much deeper than most of us think. And often overlooked.

In order to be able to love your neighbor, you must first love yourself. One follows the other in a divine metaphor, the ultimate life instruction. And yet, so many of us are filled with self-loathing, always focusing on our shortcomings and failings as we allow negative thoughts about who we are to invade our minds. For many, human love is always conditional as we keep score with everyone, especially ourselves. It is a game that creates more losers than winners. Is it any wonder why we are so unhappy? Most often, we so readily show compassion for others but sadly are often our own worse critics. Self-deprecation isn't necessarily a sign of humility. And there is a fine line between it and masochism. Scripture gives us permission to appreciate who we are just as God has created us, a temple of the Holy Spirit, and, in fact, insists that love begins with God and continues with us as we strive to let it emanate to others. No, it certainly does not mean that we are to become narcissists, who only love ourselves, and sadly, in this entitled society that is often the case. Some folks think they must love themselves exclusively, could care less about their neighbor, and have no clue who God is. Their "Golden Rule" is to do unto others before they do something to you that they don't like.

Instead, we are told to make a way for love as we are encouraged to live it. Love, which is generous, kind, and forgiving, can bind us when the world wants to tear us apart. It has always been the most powerful force on earth.

Unlike the Commandments which are filled with "shall nots," the simple principle tells us what to do to please God and shine in the world as we share this most sublime virtue. And the common word is love, the greatest Divine gift of them all.

I am back in the infusion center, getting two units of blood. This is the second time I have been the recipient of someone's unselfish donation and the enormity of the experience has moved me to tears. We are asked to be our brother's keeper, and I can't imagine a more appropriate example of that in action. The simple act of kindness is saving my life.

This current chemo protocol has been rough. I have entertained thoughts of quitting, but I suppose my will to live is still pretty strong. Most of us, given the choice between something hard that has the potential to keep us alive would choose the more difficult path. It is the way we are programmed.

I've been thinking about how somebody develops the strength and perseverance to continue when life gets tough. The history books are filled with examples of courage in the face of overwhelming odds. But I have figured out that there really is no magical formula, although perhaps it is woven into a person's DNA.

The Foundation

I have family members who were confined to Nazi concentration camps during that terrible moment in history. Some survived; others did not. I've often thought about the sheer determination, the incredible resolve it must have taken just to wake up each morning in those awful places, to cling to hope in spite of the despair, to pray for liberation to come. What a testament to the power of the human spirit!

I also have family, who, after leaving France on a promise of a potentially better life in the New World later became political pawns, spoils of war. They were removed from their homes, separated from their families and deported to parts unknown where they were despised and rejected until they finally claimed land that was deemed uninhabitable and made it their own.

My great-great grandmother came to this country from Ireland at 16 by herself. I could barely get myself to school on time at that age, but she had the courage to seek a promising future, and later, built a family on her tenacity. At the end of the Civil War, when money was tight and jobs were scarce, her husband went to work for a farmer with extensive property nearly a hundred miles away from their humble home. After months of being apart, she longed to see him, so she set off on foot with her sister and her six small children to surprise him, doing chores for families along the way in exchange for food and lodging. In six days, they had walked the incredible distance and although exhausted when they arrived, they were rewarded with a joyous reunion.

And then, there's the account of the time my grandpa hopped the tall fence that surrounded the state penitentiary to steal a bloodhound, which he had deemed to be an ideal hunting companion. Tall tale or truth? He was a master storyteller, so who knows? But it has become part of my people's folklore.

My own father spent most of World War II in the bowels of a destroyer escort as they accompanied the big naval ships into battle. It was, as he often said, his patriotic duty to serve in spite of the dangers.

I dare say that every family has a story of unimaginable bravery in the face of adversity, those who fought for a cause they believed in. I think about the human capability to adapt, to face the unthinkable, to ride the waves of heartache and despair. But I suppose that every species on this planet has had to learn to accept difficult circumstances, to adjust in order to move forward and survive. People included. Compared to our ancestors, we've got it made. We have all of the modern conveniences, the trappings of a cushy life. Has that made us soft? Perhaps. But it is important for us to remember that when put to the test, we are stronger than we think we are. The resilience of those who came before us has laid the groundwork for ours.

If you want to determine how long something will last look at its foundation. If it is solid, the building stands, even if the carpenter will not be there to witness it. As I face the most challenging time of my life, I am grateful for mine, giving me a history of strength that now, I most certainly need.

The Gratitude Lesson

I belong to several online groups of women who share the diagnosis of ovarian cancer. Collectively, we have experienced every possible complication from the disease, so the wealth of knowledge to be shared is invaluable. But there is also comfort and empathy from these women who understand the fight.

Many of my teal sisters have gone through chemo and surgery, celebrating the fact that they are considered NED (having no evidence of disease) after initial treatment. And for some of them, the disease, even in an advanced stage, never returns. They dare to even whisper the word "cured," while resuming life as they once knew it. For the lucky ones, battling cancer becomes a distant memory.

And I am envious.

It is easy to entertain thoughts of "what if," to wonder if perhaps a more skilled doctor might have taken my initial concerns over symptoms more seriously or if a radiologist with a keen eye might have identified the menacing tumor on the original scan, rather than the subsequent one taken six months later. I often question my own passivity at that time, my acceptance of what I was told rather than being my own advocate.

These are the thoughts that keep me awake at 3 a.m.

Sometimes, I even wonder if God loves those He has healed better than me. Like a petulant child, I ask The Father why He didn't choose to restore my health, too, and question if I am His least favorite. It is irrational, and a doubt-filled way to think, but suffering tends to cloud the mind with unreasonable ideas.

I suppose that it is human nature to question and compare, even if it is an exercise in futility. Undoubtedly, there are some mysteries that will remain as there are no answers. But this much I know: we have each been given a path to travel in life, a destiny to be fulfilled. And along the way, there will be difficulties. We learn about ourselves as we navigate the troubling waters, growing stronger with each obstacle overcome. Perhaps this is also where we grow our faith as we become wiser and more spiritually connected.

Certainly, I am learning to appreciate the small moments of joy, the simple pleasures. Before I became ill, I took everything for granted. That has changed. It has been almost five years since I was diagnosed, a miracle when I consider that at the beginning, when all was scary and uncertain, the determination was made that I had mere months remaining on my lifeline. That was quite the perception shift in how I viewed life. Like a kid holding a bag filled with candy, at first, it is gobbled up with wild abandon, but later, the last few pieces become precious, each bite to be savored. This is where I am now.

I am reminded of the beautiful Garden of Eden that God created for mankind. Adam and Eve were given complete dominion over this earthly paradise with the exception of the fruit of the Tree of Knowledge. Of course, we know the story: unable to resist the temptation, they committed the sin of disobedience. But I think it was much more than that; there were unappreciative for the blessings they had been given, ungracious about the miracles that surrounded them, and greedy for more. They were ungrateful. I remember that as I try not to be.

And as we celebrate the miracle of Easter, we see that early beginning in Eden come full circle as we witness the lesson that Christ's resurrection has taught us. He showed us what complete surrender through obedience looks like as he offered His body to be broken for our sins. And for those of us who are Christians, we understand the great love behind that sacrifice, which has taught us to be grateful. Regardless of where this cancer journey takes me, I am.

Perception

I am back in the infusion center. I spend a lot of time here, not particularly by choice. Two days ago, it was as though all the lights on the dashboard went out at the same time, except I am talking about my poor, overtaxed body, not my car. Labs revealed what I had already suspected: my blood has tanked. So here I sit for a series of transfusions to build me back up as I prepare for the next treatment. It seems ironic that I am being fortified only to collapse again, but I can see the light at the end of this particular tunnel. Four chemo infusions remain.

It's a long process, eight hours I've been told. And yes, I remain grateful to the kind donors whose platelets and whole blood are being pumped into my body. Some generous stranger is saving my life as I type this. Wish I could send a thank you note. I have brought snacks and my laptop. I try to write something; I need to be productive. I avoid my usual shopping sites since that time, while under the influence of steroids, I ordered four pairs of shoes. But this is a busy place with patients coming and going as the nurses push their carts from cubicle to cubicle. I am easily distracted, but I also find the people-watching fascinating, the random conversations, interesting.

And just like that, I had an idea for this blog

It is the "I" behind the eye that sees. It's an interesting phrase, one that I have repeated for so long that sometimes I believe that I coined it. I didn't. But the concept it refers to, perception, fascinates me. You see, we all most certainly view the world through a window we have individually constructed. Each pane represents something in our lives – experiences, background, gender, race, age - that affects the way we perceive everyone and everything around us. It is how we make sense of things, while shaping our philosophy of life or point of view.

And then, there is the sensory aspect. We filter what we see, touch, smell, hear, taste and assign a meaning to it based on experience. Ready for some examples? When you hear a special song from your teenage years, does it take you to that time and place? Do the smells of a certain perfume remind you of someone? Can you relate a moment of joy (or trauma) from a particular flavor or a special dish? Does watching the sunrise fill you with happiness and hope or dread? The answers to these questions are born from your own particular journey through life. I certainly will never view my health or mortality as I did a decade ago.

There is an interesting reality at work here: everything we experience is an opinion. What tastes nasty to me, may be yummy to your refined palate. What is beautiful music to me, may simply be noise to you. What stinks to me, may smell lovely to you. What is soft and comforting to your touch, may feel unnerving to me. And finally, and most important, all that we see is a perspective, not truth. It really is rather mind-boggling, isn't it?

And here is what's so remarkable. Just as you are assigning some meaning to everything and everyone you encounter, so is everybody else. EEK! We are undoubtedly influenced by the judgments, opinions, and observations of those with whom we come in contact, which serve to either confirm or cause us to second guess what we believe to be true about ourselves and society. No man (or woman) is an island. (Thank you, John Donne.) And that is why when we connect with another human soul, when we can say, "I saw that, too; I love that, too; I felt that, too;" something powerful and validating occurs. It also explains why we may meet a hundred people and only feel a kinship with one or two. Those shared experiences, shared meanings unite us, bonding us in a profound and special way. To me, it is one of the grand mysteries of life.

And so are the medical marvels that keep me alive.

The Peak End Rule

What connects us as human beings besides our bodies? Yes, we all have eyes, ears, a heart, but what about our emotions? The most obvious and idealistic answer is a laundry list of abstract terms: joy, compassion, anxiety, anger, sadness. We assume that we know how to love, and while that certainly is generally true, not every human being understands how to give and receive it. We all, however, understand pain. Whether emotional or physical, each of us understands what it feels like to hurt.

The desperation causes fear. When will it happen again? We do whatever we can to avoid it.

It's an interesting human phenomenon: while we want nothing but positive, celebratory-worthy experiences, we remember the difficult ones, the challenges and obstacles. Perhaps our brains are wired that way in an effort to caution us to tread through life carefully.

I've recently discovered the power of the "peak-end rule." When something is painful, for a sustained period of time, if the last few minutes isn't, we tend to label the experience as "not quite so bad." Memory is slippery. The more you try to hold onto it, the more elusive it is, like trying to catch a butterfly without a net. And over time, we tend to make those moments into what we want them to be because that is comfortable and reassuring.

There has been a great deal of research on how we process moments into memory. For example, if we go to a wonderful concert, but get in an accident on the way home that leaves us standing on the side of the road, waiting for a tow truck or fall in the parking lot and end up in the emergency room with a broken arm, we tend to forget the hours of toe tapping music and the pleasure it brings, choosing instead to focus on the less than desirable ending.

The quality of the pleasurable experiences we have are important, especially as we grow older or count the remaining years of our lives. I've learned that a chat with a dear friend or savoring those fruit bars I've become so fond of mean more than they did a few years ago. The small moments are significant and important. And for now, I am grabbing all of the enjoyable experiences that I can. You should, too!

What I Learned from a Puritan Poet

High school and college students, who suffered through the works of the Puritan writers in those required American Literature courses, might remember Anne Bradstreet. Or maybe not. Poems like "Upon the Burning of our House" don't exactly rank up there for its titillating imagery or thought-provoking themes. But she was, in her own right, a trailblazer, a Puritan writing poetry, at a time when such pursuits were considered quite frivolous. And need I mention that she was indeed a woman? 1642 wasn't exactly a pivotal time for women's rights, So yes, she was sort of a bad ass. But it happened accidentally.

Stay with me, I do have a point…..

I have been thinking about her lately. And yes, my random thoughts often take me to such places. In fact, she has become some sort of strange historical mentor, leading me to revisit "The Author to her Book," her poem about how she feels after becoming published. The background story is interesting. She has written poetry for her own amusement. Not daring to show it to anyone, she keeps it hidden. But when her well-meaning family finds it, they send it off to be published. Of course, she is mortified rather than thrilled, second guessing every word, every line. Her feelings of inadequacy haunt her as she doubts that her simple poems are good enough, concerned about how they will be received. (Well, she did manage to make it into every high school and college literary anthology from that time period, so I guess her works did prove to be worthy.)

So I started to wonder if every writer feels this way.

I can't speak for anybody else, but I keep telling myself that I need one last edit, one final read-through before I pull the trigger and send *Angelique's Storm* out into the world. And I wonder if I will ever be confident that it is ready for a reading public, one who will ultimately judge its worth in a most subjective way. I have to admit; it is pretty scary to turn those secret dreams into a very public reality.

We are, of course, our own worst critics, right? And as I sit here with my finger on the "send" button, I have to keep swatting the little elf perched on my shoulder who keeps whispering, "not yet." But sometimes, you have to just jump out of the plane, hoping that your parachute was properly packed… especially if you have always wanted to skydive.

Something to Leave Behind

"Everything vanishes except that which is written."

I stumbled across this quote, a simple, yet insightful comment on the human need to record the details of our world in a tangible form, to leave behind bits of ourselves for others to discover. And indeed, Archeologists have unearthed a vast cache, those written records of civilizations, on walls, in scrolls, the thoughts, experiences and ideas of a people long gone. Weren't The Ten Commandments, engraved on stone tablets, believed to have been penned by God Himself? Aren't Shakespeare's works and the epic poems of Homer and Ovid still studied and revered, noted as a thoughtful glimpse into the nature of the human mind and spirit? And in spite of the profound changes in society since the dawn of mankind, this desire to write and to share the words, has remained constant. Perhaps there is no better way to track those changes, the shifts in perception about who we are and what we think. It provides a history, a way to look back at what is important to us as a people, often providing us with a road map to navigate into the future.

Life can be fleeting. In the blink of an eye, we pass from one stage to the next, often too busy to notice the moments, both large and small. But writing allows us to capture those and to share them with others. And if we are truly brave, we make ourselves vulnerable, we tell the world what we know and feel, what we have witnessed and how it has changed us. It is a chance to form human connections on the most personal of levels. Sometimes, we take those experiences, sprinkle in a bit of imagination, building a world that only exists in the mind of the author. The tales we write bring it all to life, inspiring and entertaining the reader.

But it is more than that. Writing is a stab at immortality. I often think of what I will leave behind as I grow older and get closer to the other side. Sure, I have an attic and basement full of "treasures," things which my children will eagerly haul off to Goodwill after I have left this earth. But my stories, my journals, my (bad) poetry, will always be here, a chance for subsequent generations to know me in an intimate way. I find that rather reassuring, my legacy of words.

The Egyptians built massive pyramids to memorialize the great pharaohs. And many of the amazing manmade wonders of the world were created to pay homage to others in similar fashion. Artists create beauty, hoping it will be admired, appreciated through the ages. The desire to be remembered, to bequeath something worthwhile and meaningful, is within all of us. And so I will continue to write in the hopes that someday someone will read what I have written and think of me fondly, that somehow my life made a difference in theirs. I couldn't ask for anything more.

The Miracle

Four days ago, I anxiously sat in a crowded reception area of the radiology department of the hospital, waiting for my name to be called. Eventually, the tech led me down the long hall to the tiny room designated for PET scan patients. The nurse, who coordinates the needle sticks and dispenses the barium, waved, greeting me by name. I am a frequent flier in this place, a repeat customer. They know me here.

After sitting for an hour so that the radioactive poison could make its way through my bloodstream, I was led to the procedure room by yet another tech and instructed to lie on the narrow bed which leads into the tube of the scanner. She and I made small talk. I have a theory about this crucial part of the test. If the person who prepares you for the procedure comes out of the control room when it is all over and escorts you out, it is a good sign. They have seen the computer screen, which lights up like a Christmas tree if cancer is present. It is hard to look a person in the eye after that, to pretend that everything is fine when they know it isn't and you don't. Not everyone is a skilled actor. When she returned to announce that it was all done, I smiled. I always cling to any indication that might give me hope. Her cheerful goodbye did.

Today, I met with my medical team to get the results.

My heart raced as the doctor read the report. The large tumor lodged in my left lung is gone. The malignancies in my chest and neck lymph nodes have also disappeared. There are no longer any cancerous cells dancing around my liver. For quite some time, I have been fighting a rather large inoperable mass in the pre sacral space, which is no longer highly active and has instead been reduced to a region of indeterminate inflammation, scar tissue from a previous bowel resection and various pockets of fluid. My tumor markers have returned to normal. I began to cry.

Apparently, I am somewhat of a medical wonder. It is highly unusual for someone with stage IV cancer that has returned six times, someone who has undergone seven different unsuccessful courses of treatment with no remission, to suddenly find themselves showing no evidence of progression or metastatic disease. I am reminded that my chart approximated my life expectancy in mere months at diagnosis. That makes me quite the topic of discussion.

But they don't know my Jesus, my Great Physician. They don't understand how many prayer warriors have lifted me up, raising their voices to the heavens on my behalf. This is their miracle, too, the validation that God truly listens to those petitions whispered in earnest. He is good, always.

My love language is acts of service. I didn't realize it until recently, but I am always touched when someone does something to help me. And I will never forget the love I have felt from the many people who have walked this rocky road with me, carrying me when I was unable to take another step. They are true angels.

This afternoon, I had bloodwork following the appointment with my doctor. The nurses in the infusion center were waiting for me, anxious to share in the joy of this good news, our good news. We laughed and we cried together. They've been in the trenches with me for almost five years. And they, too, have prayed for my healing.

I will continue with chemo for three more rounds, which is six infusions, to eliminate any residual, microscopic cells. I know it won't be easy. The treatment that got me to this place is pretty brutal, but I can do it. I have a renewed resolve and a newfound strength.

I joked about booking my lecture tour to share my testimony and sing the praises of a kind and faithful God, who loves us completely and never fails us. I intend to shout my good news to anybody willing to listen. Blessings are meant to be shared.

I like to consider myself a wordsmith, but I find it difficult to truly express what I am feeling at this moment. I am grateful, so grateful. I don't know what tomorrow may bring: none of us do. But I am joyful and optimistic about tomorrow in a way I haven't allowed myself to be for almost five years.

Keep the faith, my friends. I know this much is true: each breath is a divine miracle, a precious gift. I also know that today is the first day of the rest of my life, and I fully intend to live it. Now, it is time to celebrate!

God, The Father

God created man, but He fathered woman. Yes, I know, It's a pretty bold statement to make, but it also speaks to the beauty of the remarkable relationship He designed. This is one of the many ideas I ponder on sleepless nights when my thoughts take me to some deep place. And in the morning I want to write it all down so that I won't forget, convinced that I've learned some important truth that I must share.

Eve was intended to be Adam's helpmate, and it was our Lord who, like any father-of-the-bride, offered her hand in marriage in that very first union of two souls. Yes, we know of her folly, her blatant disobedience, but even though she gave into temptation and ate the forbidden fruit, The Lord still gave her, and all women who followed, the sacred task of bringing children into the world. Eve was the first to enter into that partnership with God, becoming the mother of the human race.

Throughout the Bible, women have played pivotal roles. Esther's bravery saved her people and made her a queen; Ruth taught us about love and devotion; Miriam unselfishly put her baby son Moses in a basket to save him from certain death. Sarah and Elizabeth, considered far too old to conceive a child, gave birth to the patriarch Issac and the prophet John the

Baptist. While men left their villages, sometimes wandering for years in search of God, the women tended the home fires. They waited and watched and kept the faith. And sometimes, like the woman at the well, Jesus sought them, using the encounter to teach us, to demonstrate the mercy and grace He gives us all.

Certainly the greatest example of the central role a woman played in The Lord's Divine Plan is when the Angel Gabriel appeared to the young virgin, Mary of Nazareth, declaring that she had been chosen to give birth to The Savior of the world, the hope for all mankind. Let's face it: God could have sent Jesus to us riding on a golden unicorn with a fiery bridle. That certainly would have garnered the attention of the skeptics. But his lowly birth showed that He came to bring salvation to all, not just the rich and powerful. And we know that Jesus loved His mother. His life-long devotion to her was demonstrated throughout the Bible, from the Wedding at Cana, where He turned water into wine at her request, to the cross, where He made provisions for her care In the final moments of His life.

Three days after His death, it was a woman, Mary Magdalene, one of the earliest followers of Jesus, who was greeted by angels when she discovered the empty tomb. She was the first to share the happy news of His resurrection.

But as I think of my cancer journey, particularly my most recent miracle, I think of a common story that we all know, the raising of Lazurus from the dead and the necessary role that two women, Mary and Martha, played. The family of three were close friends of Jesus, so when Lazurus became ill, the sisters called for Him to come to their brother's bedside. But Jesus, did not appear until four days later. Lazurus was dead and Mary was inconsolable in her grief. And Jesus wept, not because of the death of His friend; He knew what the outcome would ultimately be. He cried because He knew that He would have to break Mary's heart in order to demonstrate His ability to restore a dead man's life, particularly in the presence of a group of non-believers.

His timing was perfect, just as it is now.

I'm moved by His tears of compassion which bring me comfort. I know that even if Jesus is delaying His intervention in my days of pain and sorrow, He has not forgotten me. I am promised something much more spectacular yet to come, erasing any doubt from my mind.

And as I and so many who have prayed for me waited and watched and wondered when those prayers would be answered, while I impatiently questioned if God truly listens, I tried to be still. (Not an easy task for me.) Our Lord does things in a big way to reward our patience and remind us of His great love. He makes beauty from ashes. That much I know.

This started out as an observation about how God chose women to play pivotal roles in the foundation of our faith, but I don't believe that ended with the last book of the Bible. I think He continues to use us in many ways. I see His face in so many women: the kind nurses who care for me, the girlfriends who offer their support. As our beloved Father, we are indeed His legacy. Always. And yes, even when we disappoint Him. I stand shoulder-to-shoulder with my sisters who are proud to be called daughters of The King. Don't underestimate the unyielding faith we carry in our hearts. That's what makes us strong.

My Momma Could Fold a Fitted Sheet

I recently read a magazine article written by a woman in her late twenties lamenting that "lifetime achievement awards" were only granted to older folks with long, established careers. I had to chuckle at the logic: how else can you amass a body of work significant enough to merit recognition if you haven't lived?

When I think of growing older, my thoughts turn to my mother. To me, she was quite beautiful, reminding me of Polly Bergen, a starlet in the 60's. (Google her.) Of course, she never saw herself that way, saying that beauty is a burden because it is fleeting. I was skeptical: as an awkward teenager, I was willing to chance it to have the power to open doors with just a smile. (Yes, I blatantly stole that line.) But as I grew older, I understood the permanence of more important things, like values and skills. She taught me that kindness, along with a sense of humor, were much more powerful. I try to remember that.

Momma was a planner. She kept a calendar filled projects that she aspired to complete, and she made a to-do list that she kept on the kitchen counter to be reviewed each morning over a cup of strong black coffee. By the end of the day, she noted what she had accomplished as she anticipated what was to follow. When she passed away, I found baby blankets she had lovingly crocheted in a bin labeled "to my future great grandchildren." I cried over that discovery. And in many ways, I am like her in that regard. I tend to look ahead, a skill I fine-tuned once I became a mother myself and was charged with the task of keeping young humans alive. Yep, Momma could do anything, including the superhuman ability to fold a fitted sheet. Her linen closet was an organized thing of beauty. Unfortunately, she didn't pass skill that along to me. I gave up trying to create a neat little package ages ago.

It's hard not to look in the mirror and recognize the way cancer has changed me, my face a roadmap of experience. Age and chemo can be a pretty transformative tool and not in a good way. But then, I hear the words from my mother: the only advantage to aging, she would say, is that it gives you a past, a big story to tell, filled with happy and sad times. And I agree. We are all working on an autobiography, one chapter at a time.

She taught me a lot, and I am grateful for those lessons.

And my advice to those young women? Be patient. Life happens, the years passing by far too quickly. And if you are lucky, someday you will have a lifetime to celebrate, too.

The Broken Vase

When my son was a toddler, we accompanied a friend on a visit to one of her friends. We were in the neighborhood, and it was one of those spontaneous decisions, a drop-in visit that you would only consider doing with somebody with whom you have a close relationship.

She graciously welcomed us into her beautifully decorated home, and I quickly surveyed the room for potential disasters at the tiny hands of my inquisitive little boy. I think they call that intuition, but every mother knows how quickly such things can happen. Our hostess, sensing my apprehension, assured me that although she had no children, she often entertained small ones and that nothing was off limits. I tried to relax.

I think we had been there all of ten minutes when my son walked over to a rather large ornate, obviously valuable, vase and without hesitating, pushed it onto the floor where it shattered into hundreds of tiny pieces. There was a long moment of silence and then the loud wailing of baby tears.

Unsure of what to do, I immediately began to gather the shards of glass with one hand while trying to prevent a toddler meltdown with the other, all the while muttering my apologies. I could feel my cheeks turning red, my embarrassment palpable.

"I'm so sorry," I said. "I should have had been paying attention. Please let me know where you bought it so that I can replace this for you."

She simply smiled. "That's not necessary. It's old, something I've had for years."

Dang. My kid had just destroyed some precious family heirloom.

"Don't give it another thought," she said.

The next day I sent her flowers, which I considered a small consolation prize for what she had lost. But I don't think she realized what a priceless gift she had given me that day. She readily and sincerely forgave, all the while allowing me to save face. I was incredibly grateful.

And that lesson has stayed with me. Many years later, I had a coworker come to visit. As we sat in the "preacher's parlor," a rarely used formal room where all the tchotchkes were displayed, her son casually walked over to a low table and reached for an ornate figurine that had belonged to my mother. Before either of us could stop him, he had picked it up and, misjudging the weight, let it slip through his little fingers. We both stared in disbelief as slivers of porcelain lay scattered across the floor. She scooped the child up in her arms and scolded him. He began to cry at this mother's displeasure while I ran to get the broom and dustpan.

"Please don't worry about it," I said, fully understanding how uncomfortable she was. "Children are inquisitive and that was an inexpensive trinket." I hugged them for good measure.

Her face softened. "Thanks," she whispered.

Life is somewhat circular. What goes around often does indeed come around in ironic ways. But sometimes, that becomes a lesson in grace, an opportunity to maintain respect for oneself and others. Those moments are golden.

The Road Traveled

―――――・❦・―――――

A few weeks into my initial treatment, I made the mistake of asking Mr. Google about my odds of survival. Ovarian cancer, especially at Stage IV, is relatively aggressive, resistant to chemotherapy and known to recur far too quickly. Perhaps it was a form of self-torture, but I wanted a number, something objective. In those early days, as I swam in a big sea of uncertainty, I researched like crazy, looking for a glimmer of hope from some random website. Instead, I was given a frightening dose of reality by the American Cancer Society: my chances of being alive five years after diagnosis was a mere 17%.

I tried not to think of that as days turned into months, as each scan delivered disappointing news. I readily agreed to surgeries and one form of treatment after another, refusing to give up the fight. And all the while, I kept a firm grip on that elusive companion called hope.

I wrote as often as I could, compiling these little snippets of my experience until I had enough for a book. Somehow, I had convinced myself that preserving these moments was important. Perhaps that gave me purpose.

But today is significant. It is my 5th "cancerversary," a coined word to acknowledge the victory of endurance. This marks an important chapter in the story of my life, one that confirms my status as a survivor. I am mighty grateful to still be here.

Mr. Google doesn't know everything.

The Power of the Moment

There is a state of being where that little voice in your head goes haywire. It comments, speculates, judges, compares, complains, and whines. It imagines everything that can go wrong in living Technicolor as the mental movie plays over and over again on a nonstop reel. This is called worry. Yes, it is irrational, often based on nothing more than a feeling. And we all know how fickle those can be. But I have lived there for the past few weeks as I have worked to get this book ready for release. I agonized over typos, wondered if my words rang true, speculated over how it would be received by readers. It became a nasty little game of self-torture, sprinkled with a healthy dose of self-doubt and second-guessing.

Whew. That felt good to admit in public. I think perhaps that sometimes we are so busy pretending to be confident, to be in charge of all things, even those clearly out of our control, that we become like actors on a stage as we don the mask and whisper, "everything is just fine." But let's face it: human nature is such that whenever we embark on something important, it is bound to be scary, accompanied by a bit of apprehension. And it isn't a bad thing, unless we are unable to ultimately tame the beast.

I had a profound thought as I was lying awake one night, wondering if the manuscript was ready or if I should edit it one more time. What good would it do for me to become so anxiety-riddled that I failed to enjoy the moment, missed the exhilaration of the experience of sending the book out into the world? I mean, after all, wasn't that the whole point of writing it, to share my experience at this, the most vulnerable time of my life? At the risk of sounding like a song from a Disney movie, it was time to "let it go," and hopefully to let it thrive and grow.

Much of the pain and angst we experience is self-inflicted. We become mired in the past, which we cannot change or fret about the future which hasn't yet happened. Somehow, the present gets bookended between the two and is lost. And quite frankly, this bit of time is all we have. That's probably the most important lesson I have learned: the realization of the importance of enjoying what is happening right now is pretty powerful.

I launched a book today. I closed my eyes and imagined that people are reading it, allowing my words to enter their consciousness and hoping that all I have shared will touch their hearts. I didn't worry about the outcome. I am just appreciating this moment. And I am mighty grateful for it and all of you who have chosen to read it.

May you greet every sunrise with joy and anticipation. May you find contentment in the simplest of experiences. And may every day of your life be BEAUTEALFUL because it is indeed a most precious gift.

Author's Notes:

On the day that I was diagnosed, I walked out of the doctor's office and slipped into the closest ladies' room. As I stood, staring at my reflection in the mirror I knew that life as I had once known it would never be the same. Cancer changes everything.

It is difficult not to panic, not to allow the imagination to run wild with "what ifs," when you are given bad news. It's like being attacked by all of those bullets we have spent a lifetime dodging.

But struggle also create opportunity. For me, the pressing question was not if I would survive, but what would I do with the experience. It weighed heavily on my mind during those first days of disbelief. Since I already had a blog space where I occasionally posted, I figured that it would be a good place to openly share what I was bound to learn along the way. I hoped that in the process I could help somebody else.

I was once told that so much of my writing is too faith-focused. I think that it was meant to be a criticism, but I quickly responded with a "thank you." I can't imagine how anyone can stare into the steely eyes of the Grim Reaper and not question what they believe or wonder what lies beyond this life. Being aware of one's own mortality provides fertile ground for those personal convictions to grow. In the still of the night, when fear haunted me like some ever-present ghoul, the whispered prayers calmed my spirit and gave me peace. I have learned where my true north is. Illness became the door through which I traveled into the baptismal, as ironically, I was born again into a place where God most certainly lives.

And I am happy to be here.

Looking back at the road I've traveled:

Year One – The diagnosis, Stage IV ovarian cancer, was followed by a whirlwind of medical appointments. Eighteen chemo infusions and major surgery got me to NED status. No evidence of disease: the four most beautiful words in the English language. My hair is growing back dark, thick and curly.

Year Two – The beast has returned, and I am in warrior mode. Surgery, followed by chemo. I've been told that I will lose my hair again.

Year Three – Chemo, chemo and more chemo – They were right: I am bald. The good news is that it worked, and I got a clear scan. I've been placed on a PARP inhibitor, which is supposed to be a breakthrough in the treatment of ovarian cancer. Although it was not without side effects, I was thrilled to be freed from the chemo chair for a few months.

Year Four – Cancer is relentless, and after a PET scan confirmed a recurrence, I've been scheduled for major surgery. The hospitals are on lockdown because of COVID, and I am alone for six days. It was the worst of times. I was placed on another PARP inhibitor, but that was short-lived after several severe reactions. I am back on chemo, this time dancing with "the red devil" as it is called and its platinum-based cousin. I had a partial response to treatment.

Year Five – The decision was made to try immunotherapy, a daily pill and two infusions every three weeks. It was the easiest treatment of all, but it was ineffective. The cancer has metastasized to my lung and lymph nodes. I've tried not to panic. And now, I'm back in chemo, the tough one they use as a "last resort." But it is working, and I am in remission, which is unheard of for someone with my medical history. Frankly, I am much more partial to the word "miracle." I will be on this treatment for an indefinite period of time. It's not what I had hoped for, but it's a small price to pay for a few more tomorrows. And I remain grateful.

What's next? Only God knows, but I am filled with hope and optimism. And each day is truly a gift.

Y'all be blessed.

Other Books by Paula Millet:

Cosigning a Lie
Angelique's Storm
Angelique's War
Angelique's Peace
Angelique's Legacy
Ovacoming
Still Ovacoming

Made in the USA
Columbia, SC
22 June 2022